AMELIA EARHART
The Final Story

AMELIA EARHART
The Final Story

Vincent V. Loomis

with Jeffrey L. Ethell

Random House · New York

Grateful acknowledgment is made to the following for permission to reprint previously published material:

Beacon Press: Excerpts from LETTERS FROM AMELIA, by Jean L. Backus, Beacon Press, Boston, 1982.

Doubleday & Company, Inc.: Excerpt from HOLLYWOOD PILOT, by Don Dwiggins. Copyright © 1967 by Don Dwiggins. Reprinted by permission of Doubleday & Co., Inc.

Harcourt Brace Jovanovich, Inc. and Harrap Limited: Excerpts from SOARING WINGS: A BIOGRAPHY OF AMELIA EARHART, copyright 1939 by George Palmer Putnam; renewed 1967 by Margaret H. Lewis. Reprinted by permission of Harcourt Brace Jovanovich, Inc., and Harrap Limited, London (the publishers). Excerpts from LAST FLIGHT by Amelia Earhart, copyright 1937 by George Palmer Putnam; renewed 1965 by Mrs. George Palmer Putnam. Reprinted by permission of Harcourt Brace Jovanovich, Inc.

Elinor Smith: Excerpt from AVIATRIX, by Elinor Smith, Harcourt Brace Jovanovich, New York, 1981.

Library of Congress Cataloging in Publication Data
Loomis, Vincent V.
  Amelia Earhart, the final story.
  Bibliography: p.
  Includes index.
  1. Earhart, Amelia, 1897–1937.   2. Air pilots—
United States—Biography.   I. Ethell, Jeffrey L.
II. Title.
TL540.E3L66   1985   629.13′092′4 [B]   84-42531
ISBN 0-394-53191-4

To my wife, Georgette Loomis, who took part in all my expeditions and to our children, all eight of them, and their families.

To Tom Gurney, Jr., for his support and adventurous spirit.

To all members who participated in each of our Earhart expeditions.

Vincent V. Loomis

Contents

Introduction

EARHART DISAPPEARS! LADY LINDY LOST!

THE headlines of July 2, 1937, dramatically reported the end of an era. Amelia Earhart and her navigator, Frederick Noonan, had mysteriously vanished while undertaking yet another assault on aviation records in the bold, courageous and sometimes foolhardy manner of pilots of the time.

From then on, fewer pioneering flights would be made with Old World nautical navigation techniques; new breakthroughs in radio navigation had produced effective yet expensive black boxes. Thereafter, such flights would seldom be undertaken by "stunt" fliers; rather, they would be sponsored by the government or by large corporations that could supply the funds. Sadly, for many the romance of aviation's Golden Age vanished with Amelia Earhart.

From the moment Amelia's airplane, a Lockheed Electra, disappeared, controversy and rumor continued to dominate stories about the fate of the two pioneers. Did they run out of fuel looking for tiny Howland Island, their intended destination southwest of Honolulu, and then ditch in the vast Pacific Ocean? Were they on a secret government spy mission over the Japanese mandated islands, which were then being fortified? Did the Electra crash-land in the Marshall Islands, on Hull Island, on some other small island or even on Saipan? If so, did the flyers survive to be captured by the Japanese and eventually suffer death by execution or disease? Were they detained by the Japanese as spies, then kept in secret as bargaining chips in the event that war with the U.S. broke out? Did they survive the war, an embarrassment to both the Japanese and the U.S. governments, forced to live out their lives in obscurity? What are the real answers? What is the real story?

Numerous books, articles and even movies have, over the years, attempted to solve the mystery. "Earhart fever" has haunted many people, driving them to devote their energies to uncovering the truth. Conjecture, theory and controversy appear in print year after year. Wire services still look for copy dealing with the Earhart disappearance, one of the ten leading news stories of all time.

Through tenacious research and years of effort, we have slowly traced what happened to Amelia Earhart and Fred Noonan. In an attempt to avoid hearsay and hypotheses, we have gone after first-person interviews and hard documentation. Traveling to the Marshall Islands time after time, we slowly gained the confidence of a reserved and cloistered people. Some were still very much afraid of the Japanese; some remained loyal to them.

Research was done in the official archives of the United States and Japan, and interviews were conducted with many of Earhart's contemporaries and with former Japanese naval personnel. In the interest of narrative clarity, some of our discoveries have not been related in chronological order; however, the content of each episode has not been changed.

Pinpointing where the Electra actually was at the moment radio contact was lost with the Coast Guard cutter *Itasca* was crucial to substantiating where Earhart could have crashed. Former Pan American Airways radio operator Paul Rafford, Jr., with over forty years of experience ranging from the Clippers to working with the NASA astronaut recovery team, reconstructed that last flight with amazing accuracy.

Secret Japanese diplomatic message traffic was found in Tokyo, at last revealing what happened in high places during those tense weeks and months after the Electra disappeared.

At the National Air and Space Museum, Smithsonian Institution, Paul Garber, Phil Edwards, Jay Spenser and Claudia Oakes were more than helpful in providing original documentation and photographs from the museum's rich files. Larry Webb spent many hours copying and printing many of the photos seen in these pages.

Credit for the final manuscript's making its way into print goes to our Random House editor, Robert D. Loomis, who would not let the story be sidetracked, and to Mike Marcon, master story-teller and author, who worked for months shaping the narrative.

Here, after years of effort, is the final story.

Vincent V. Loomis

Jeffrey L. Ethell

Prologue:

An Incident of Little Consequence

VINCE LOOMIS: 1952

THE Marshall Islands are stunning in their beauty, but I couldn't help thinking to myself, "Vince, let's get this insanity over with and go home!" As a career United States Air Force officer with two tours of duty in the South Pacific flying Douglas C-47 "Gooney Birds," I had had enough of the vast stretches of ocean. But my experience, particularly over the Marshalls, had fitted me for a unique job. On 11 September 1952, I was issued RESTRICTED Special Orders for Task Group 132.4. In preparation for the atomic bomb tests under Operation Ivy, six Air Force enlisted men, one Marshallese civilian and I were to erect visual navigation aids.

Flying over the atolls in the Pacific produces an eerie sense of never quite knowing where one is. Getting lost is a very real possibility unless headings and drift are continually monitored. The Marshallese themselves are known as expert navigators, able to travel hundreds of miles between islands in small outriggers by observing the changing shapes of the waves. Their method never made any sense to me, but then, I did not have a heritage of hundreds of years of open-ocean seafaring. My training had been in the rushed Army Air Force days of World War II, when pilots and navigators were turned out like pancakes.

During the Operation Ivy tests someone had come up with the idea of helping American aviators by placing colored marker panels on selected islands. A codebook in the cockpit would show a pilot that if, for example, he saw a red/blue/green panel below, he was over Rongerik Atoll. After the atomic tests, the canvas panels would be left for the Marshallese, who could use them for whatever purposes they wished. I had the job of erecting these panels with the help of my crew.

On September 16 we embarked on LST 836 at Eniwetok Atoll, about 700 miles south-southwest of Wake Island. Lieutenant M. J. Walker, USN, the commander of 836, greeted the eight of us and showed us below to our quarters. Though the ship was cramped, it accommodated all of us quite well. I was surprised at how much an LST could hold, including two smaller landing craft, LCVPs, similar to the LST, with a ramp that dropped down in front to allow the unloading of material onto the beach.

By September 20 we had reached Bikini Atoll, and we proceeded to Rongelap Atoll at daybreak under SECRET orders at full speed, 10 knots. As our interpreter, Kinsu Glass, a Marshallese native from Kwajalein Atoll, did our talking for us with the locals, we began erecting the panels. By the twenty-first we were finished there and under way for Rongerik Atoll, where we anchored at sunset.

The process continued. From atoll to island, we would chug up to the beach and wade ashore.

On the morning of the twenty-fifth we were off Ujae Atoll. At 8:49 A.M. LCVP #1, one of our small landing craft, was launched. We chugged up to the beach, lowered the ramp and walked out onto the sand just like Douglas MacArthur.

After picking up the atoll chief, we headed for one of the uninhabited islands about ten miles away, where we beached the LCVP. As we organized ourselves and got the panel markers out, we came across an old shoe near the shoreline. It had been there for some time; it was thoroughly weatherbeaten and bent out of shape to the point one could not tell if it was a man's or a woman's shoe. All of us thought this was surely the most unlikely place to find a remnant of civilization, but it was only of passing interest so we tossed it aside.

Trekking across the tiny island, trying to pick the best spot for the panels, we found an airplane covered by coral and vegetation. We did not notice it in the dense overgrowth until we were within a few feet of the fuselage. Looking back the way we had come, we could see that years ago a swath had been cleared from the shoreline to the center of the island where the aircraft had been dragged and covered. There was no sign that it had crash-landed where it now lay.

Our curiosity was aroused enough to have Kinsu ask the native chief if he knew the machine to be American or Japanese. The chief had visited the island infrequently and was reluctant to express himself, but his impression seemed to be that it was Japanese. Despite this, one of my airmen asked if it could be the plane belonging to Amelia Earhart, who had disappeared before World War II. Others remarked that it couldn't have been hers, since she supposedly went down at some other remote spot in the Pacific.

At the time, the incident seemed of little or no consequence—I'm afraid that even as a pilot I didn't really care what type of aircraft it was. I was concerned with our tight time schedule: the H-bomb test was not far off, and our visits to the atolls were strictly timed by the tides. The effort there was also taking more time and energy than planned, due to the undergrowth that we went to considerable trouble to clear.

Soon we were back in the company of Lieutenant Walker, and our landing craft was hoisted aboard 836. We finished our work on Ujae on September 26. The covered airplane had already left my thoughts as we started the long cruise back for Eniwetok. I was concerned only with getting the atomic testing over with and returning stateside. The thought of testing on the home islands of these lovely people sickened me. For all I knew, I would never return.

AMELIA EARHART
The Final Story

Chapter 1

Last Takeoff

*I*T must have been a welcome sight. When the runway popped into view, the sometimes crackling tension between Fred and Amelia subsided, and exhaustion turned to smiles as the Electra's landing gear locked down. For the moment, the cramped cabin of the twin-engine airplane became a friendlier place as Amelia struggled to maintain that last few seconds of vigilance she needed to get her large, droning airplane safely on the ground at 3:00 P.M. on June 29, 1937.

Engines on big airplanes seem to run best when there is land beneath them. The dirty little airstrip that stretched ahead into the jungle soothed the "automatic rough," the nerve-tearing skips and misses that engines mysteriously develop when land slides beneath, out of sight, and endless water is all one sees.

"It's a very big ocean—*so* much water!" Amelia Earhart, worn and exhausted, must have wanted desperately to see her husband, George Putnam, again. As her plane's wheels bounced along the rutted, dusty runway at Lae, New Guinea, she was probably beginning to feel that she just might.

The next day, safely on the ground, she wrote in her log (published after her disappearance as *Last Flight*), "After a flight of seven hours and forty-three minutes from Port Darwin, Australia, against headwinds as usual, my Electra now rests on the shores of the Pacific. Beyond the Gulf of Huon the waters stretch into the distance. Somewhere beyond the horizon lies California. Twenty-two thousand miles have been covered so far. There are 7000 more to go."

Lae was an ideal jumping-off spot for both crew and aircraft. It was headquarters for the Guinea Airways Company, which flew a Lockheed 10, a sister craft to the Lockheed Electra, and service for the Earhart "flying laboratory" would be excellent. The airstrip itself was cut out of 3000 feet of jungle on the edge of a cliff overlooking the ocean. Accommodations for Amelia and Fred at the local hotel, designed by European companies working the gold mines, were ideal for resting before the longest leg of the trip. She wrote, "Food, hot baths, mechanical service, radio and weather reports, advice from veteran pilots here—all combine to make us wish we could stay."

The first night Amelia had dinner with the manager of Guinea Airways, Eric Chaters, while Fred, James A. Collopy, district superintendent of civil aviation in New Guinea, and some others stayed at the hotel to take advantage of the variety of refreshments available. Chaters noticed that things were not going well between pilot and navigator. Fred had started drinking heavily again.

Throughout the next day the Guinea Airways mechanics went over the Electra, cleaning the spark plugs, changing the engine oil and cleaning the oil filters, working on a fluctuating fuel pump, repairing the Sperry Gyro Horizon and running the engines to check them. Earhart was hoping that the mechanics could get everything done so that she and Fred could leave on July 1. She was feeling increasing pressure from her husband's cables to get to Oakland, California, by July 4 to keep several dates for public appearances that he had made for her.

As the morning of July 1 passed, however, it became obvious that the flight would not get under way. The all-important chronometers, essential for precise celestial navigation, had not been set because the exact-time radio signals broadcast by the U.S. Navy and the Bureau of Standards had not been picked up by either the Electra's radios or the excellent receivers at Lae. Too, the weather was deteriorating, and the wind direction would have forced a dangerous takeoff headed inland with full fuel (a takeoff toward the ocean would provide a safer, longer, low climb out with no obstacles). The wait continued.

While Amelia and Fred toured the New Guinea countryside in a truck borrowed from the hotel manager, the Guinea Airways mechanics finished servicing the Electra. The errant fuel pump was fixed and back up to proper pressure. After everything was pronounced ready, 1100 gallons of 90-octane fuel and 64 gallons of fresh oil were pumped aboard. According to Collopy, "One tank contained only 50 gallons of its total capacity of 100 gallons. This tank contained 100 octane fuel and they considered 50 gallons of this fuel sufficient for the take-off from Lae." This higher-than-normal-octane fuel would allow the engines to develop more power—much needed for the overweight takeoff.

Twenty-five hundred miles away, the U.S. Coast Guard cutter *Itasca*, with Commander Warner K. Thompson as captain, was standing by near Howland Island to shepherd the Electra in. Aboard ship many had grave doubts about the ability of the Electra's crew to operate their radios properly, for Amelia was planning to use frequencies not suitable for radio direction-finding.

The invention of the direction finder (DF) had been a major breakthrough in aviation. Instead of trying to follow deduced compass headings over measured distances or performing complex celestial navigation fixes, air crews could now be pointed to their final destination by tuning their DF radio to a certain frequency and aligning a loop antenna by listening for the weakest reception, or "null," which would indicate a bearing to fly to their destination. If there was a DF on the ground, its operators could tune in to an aircraft's radio transmissions, get a bearing and relay that to the crew by voice communication.

However, there were definite limitations to using DFs. First, the bearing obtained from the loop antenna did not tell at which end of the indicator needle the radio source was located—front or back—since the needle did not point. It simply aligned itself with the loop. And although most radios could pick up a range of frequencies, only the lower end of the frequency band provided signals strong enough to give a bearing at a distance. If the signals were too weak, then a radioman could not use them for direction-finding. If a DF was to be used successfully, transmissions would have to be made between 250 and 600 kilocycles, and the operator would have to transmit for about two minutes to allow the DF antenna to be rotated properly and "home" in.

Though effective, DF operation was an art that had to be studied and mastered before its benefits could be realized. It was far more complex than simply talking into a microphone on any frequency and expecting a steer to be given.

Days before, on June 21, as Amelia was flying from Singapore to Java, the *Itasca* had passed a message through Coast Guard headquarters in Washington: "Advise Earhart from Darwin she will communicate with *Itasca* via Samoa the desired frequency, time and type of signal best for her homing device. She will advise fully via Samoa before leaving Lae." Thompson was asking Amelia to send him a message about how she wished to home in on Howland with radio, then confirm with another message before leaving Lae. The tortuous route these messages for Earhart from the *Itasca* had to travel, because of radio relay requirements, was to Tutuila in the Samoas; to Suva, Fiji; to Sydney, Australia; to Darwin; to Rabaul, New Guinea; to Salamaua; to Lae.

The message went unanswered and was repeated the next day.

Again, on June 23, the *Itasca* had the request passed on to Amelia, asking her to designate the time and type of radio signals desired. The cutter advised also that "we will give smoke by day and searchlight by night." The next day the *Itasca* received a message from the Coast Guard's San Francisco Division. Amelia's husband, George, had requested the ship adjust its radio transmitter "for possible use of 3105 kilocycles for voice," but reported that the Lockheed's direction finder covered a range of only "200 to 1400 kilocycles."

Coast Guard officials were thoroughly confused.

To further complicate matters, from Saurabaya, Java, where the Electra was being worked on before the flights to Australia and Lae, Amelia sent a message through the radio net to the *Itasca* that her DF homing device "covers 200 to 1500 and 2400 to 4800 kilocycles but not near the end bands." To the bewilderment of the *Itasca* radiomen, she then asked the ship to transmit the letter A, the cutter's position, and its call letters every half hour on 7500 kilocycles, a frequency well above the tuning range of the Electra's DF. This frequency was effective for long-distance communication but was completely unusable by airborne

DFs. Not only were Earhart and her husband requesting different frequencies of the *Itasca*, but apparently Amelia was not getting the ship's messages or did not understand them.

The frequency she must have had in mind was 750 meters (400 kilocycles)—she was obviously muddled about the difference between meters and kilocycles. Curiously enough, she had managed to get it right when she requested 400 kilocycles from the Coast Guard cutter *Ontario*, standing midway between Lae and Howland, but then erred again when she requested 900 kilocycles from the USS *Swan*, stationed halfway between Howland and Hawaii. Such a frequency should not have been used for direction-finding, being in the middle of the AM broadcast band. What she actually wanted was 900 meters (333 kilocycles), a channel frequently used for communication and direction-finding between ships and aircraft in the 1930s

Itasca advised Earhart on June 28 that the ship's DF reception frequency range was 270 to 550 kilocycles. Later she radioed that she understood the ship would be voicing on 3105 kilocycles with a long continuous signal on her approach—it was as if she had not even received the *Itasca*'s message. Again Earhart was asking for a frequency that would be quite weak for direction-finding, but the ship's radio personnel had no choice but to accept what Earhart was asking for. They advised her that they would comply with the request.

Commander Thompson and the men of the *Itasca* were finding the lack of coordination and the odd frequency requests not only confusing but maddening. How could there be such a dearth of common sense when two lives depended upon proper use of radios in the air and at sea? Adding to Thompson's frustration, there were too many high-ranking officials telling him what to do—his superiors in San Francisco, the U.S. Navy, and now Department of the Interior representative Richard B. Black, who was aboard the *Itasca*.

Black had been responsible for having the runways constructed on Howland before Amelia and Fred left the States, and against Thompson's protests, he made sure an experimental Navy high-frequency DF would be set up on Howland as a backup to the *Itasca*'s. The Coast Guard captain was afraid it would only add to the confusion. Both the DF on the *Itasca* and the one at Howland were more than capable of getting a bearing when Amelia "voiced," or talked over her radio—but only if she was on the proper frequency. Assuming two-way voice radio contact between aircraft and ship, *Itasca* operators could easily relay the bearing to her and she could fly it inbound to Howland by following a simple compass heading.

One final time, on June 29, Commander Thompson radioed Earhart, now at Lae, asking her to advise the ship twelve hours before leaving Lae and to confirm the frequencies desired. Her reply was again confusing.

While the aircraft was being serviced, Amelia and Fred repacked the Electra to eliminate everything not essential to the flight. "We have even discarded as much personal property as we can decently get along without and henceforth propose to travel lighter than ever before," wrote Amelia. "All Fred has is a small tin case which he picked up in Africa. I notice it still rattles, so it cannot be packed very full."

On the evening of July 1, the night before the takeoff from Lae, the two fliers were to retire early, but Fred decided to spend the time drinking with his friends. The next morning, July 2, Fred made it back to his hotel room only forty-five minutes before Amelia came pounding on his door to announce they would take off in a couple of hours. According to his drinking cronies of the previous night, Fred had complained of the strenuous pace set for him by Amelia, and found that as good a reason as any for seeking the comforts of the bottle.

Harry Balfour, the radio operator at Lae, recalled, "Noonan . . . was on a bender up at Bulolo during the time and was put on board with a bad hangover and she [Earhart] did remark to me in the radio station the night previous that she wished she could have taken me as radio operator because neither of them could read Morse and therefore could not get navigational assistance from land based radio stations or shipping."

When her husband's last wire arrived at Lae, querying Amelia about the cause of the delay, she wired back a terse "Crew unfit."

Balfour recalled also that "she unloaded all her surplus equipment on me including her pistol and ammunition, books, letters and facility books; her radio equipment was pre-flight checked." The Guinea Airways radio operator found it hard to believe that such a flight was going to be made with so little regard for proper use of the radio and with an incapacitated navigator. He determined he would do all he could for Amelia short of getting on the aircraft with her.

Weather information was sent to the Fleet Air Base in Honolulu from several stations and passed on to Balfour at Lae: there were southeast winds from 18 to 25 knots to the *Ontario*, midway between Lae and Howland; from there to Howland, winds from the east-northeast at 15 to 20 knots; heavy rain squalls were predicted on the route of flight in the area three hundred miles east of Lae with scattered heavy showers and some cumulus buildups for the remainder of the flight; and *Itasca* weather indicated generally east winds at 10 knots.

Just before takeoff that morning, Earhart sent the same confounding radio request to the *Itasca* that she had sent several days earlier from Saurabaya—to transmit on 7500 kilocycles. She did not indicate she was taking off immediately, but said, "I will give long calls by voice on 3105 kilocycles at a quarter after and a quarter to the hour." She was acting as if all of the *Itasca*'s previous messages had somehow disappeared before reaching her.

Strangely, there was also a mystery about just what radio equipment was installed in the Electra. No one aboard the *Itasca* seemed to know that the trailing wire antenna so crucial for the Electra's 500-kilocycle emergency frequency had been left back in the United States along with the telegraph key; Amelia and Fred considered these useless instruments, since neither of them was proficient with Morse code. They failed to consider that a telegraph key could send out a clear signal (compared to voice transmissions) that could be picked up by other DFs.

At one point, when the *Itasca* requested George Putnam to list the equipment in his wife's aircraft, he could give no accurate information. As Commander Thompson later recalled, "Viewed from the fact that Miss Earhart's flight was largely dependent upon radio communication, her attitude toward arrangements was most casual, to say the least."

During preparations for the July 2 takeoff, the Lae radio operator, Harry Balfour, conveyed to Amelia his increasing uneasiness about the next leg of the flight—the confusion over radio frequencies, a sick navigator, and the dumping of vital survival gear. Balfour decided that after takeoff they would maintain voice radio contact on her "day frequency" of 6210 kilocycles as long as possible.

After Fred was helped aboard the Electra, Amelia climbed in through the cockpit hatch; the engines were started and warmed up, and she taxied the plane carefully to the end of the runway. The Electra was dangerously heavy with fuel. Guinea Airways Electra pilots watching remarked that it would take some top-notch flying to get the plane into the air.

The night before, she had written in her log, "Not much more than a month ago I was on the other shore of the Pacific, looking westward. This evening, I looked eastward over the Pacific. In those fast-moving days which have intervened, the whole width of the world has passed behind us—except this broad ocean. I shall be glad when we have the hazards of its navigation behind us."

Commander Thompson spent the entire day she was supposed to leave Lae trying to confirm that she had, in fact, taken off. His message requesting a twelve-hour prior notification of Amelia's takeoff had only prompted the same confusing reply about frequencies, but did not acknowledge his request for her time of departure. Finally Harry Balfour at Lae did confirm that, conveniently, she was off at 0000 Greenwich time, which translated to 10:00 A.M. local time at Lae. Greenwich Civil Time was used to avoid confusion over the frequent time-zone passages; if she were to report she was over a certain point at 0650 Greenwich (or GCT) that would mean she was 6 hours and 50 minutes into the flight, and the time could be converted correctly into local time anywhere.

Amelia swung the Electra around, pointed it down Lae's runway, pushed both throttles forward and headed toward the ocean. The jungle greenery passed beneath her, and as she dropped below the rim of the cliff at the edge of the runway, the heavy Electra slanted toward the water stretching out ahead.

Jim Collopy, who was watching and almost holding his breath, recalled, "The take-off was hair-raising. After taking every yard of the 1000 yard runway from the northwest end of the aerodrome towards the sea, the aircraft had not left the ground 50 yards from the end of the runway. When it did leave, it sank away but was by this time over the sea. It continued to sink to about five or six feet above the water and had not climbed more than 100 feet before it disappeared from sight. In spite of this, however, it was obvious that the aircraft was well handled, and pilots of Guinea Airways who have flown Lockheed aircraft were loud in their praise of the take-off with such an overload."

Pilot Bertie Heath was inbound to Lae, returning from one of his regular runs to the gold fields. From his cockpit he could see the field and noted the wind was calm because the dust from the dirt road that the Electra had crossed at the end of the runway "didn't disperse quickly, just sort of hung there."

The propellers sliced at the tops of minueting whitecaps, throwing great plumes of salt spray back over the engines. Fighting with all her might, Amelia managed to retain control and in the process begin a very shallow climb. The Electra was now outbound on a straight-line course for Howland, or so most of the world believed. Within 18 hours, if all went well, it would be circling Howland for landing.

One hour after takeoff, Earhart contacted Harry Balfour on 6210 kilocycles, her day frequency. Four hours later Amelia reported to him that she was cruising at 10,000 feet but was reducing altitude owing to thick banks of cumulus clouds.

Shortly after sunset (7 hours and 20 minutes into the flight) she called in again to inform Harry that she was at 7000 feet and making 150 knots, and she was going to change to her night frequency of 3105 kilocycles. Balfour immediately responded, urging her not to switch because her signal was still very strong.

Either she did not hear him—or ignored his advice. Harry Balfour never heard from her again, and indeed Earhart never had two-way radio communication with anyone again. When Balfour received a "winds aloft" message from Ocean Island (almost directly on the Electra's flight path) advising of strong headwinds, he was unable to raise her on either frequency to pass on the valuable information.

The *Ontario*, between Lae and Howland, had not heard from Amelia at all. Those aboard the ship were perplexed—either she was so far off schedule she could not be heard, or she was lost.

The *Itasca* sat lazing in the swells just off Howland Island. If all went as originally planned, Earhart would arrive around sunrise. The crew was ready. Commander Thompson walked the narrow confines of the ship's passageways, letting his men know what he expected of them. In spite of Earhart's failure to make sense in her previous messages of the past several days, Thompson was determined to help her find the island. At daybreak he wanted plenty of thick, black smoke sent up by the ship's firemen so that at least she'd have something to see on the horizon.

In the ship's radio room Chief Radioman Bellarts looked at the big sweep-hand clock on the bulkhead. It was 1418 GCT, 1:48 in the morning at Howland. She had been airborne more than 14 hours.

He pressed his earphones closer as Earhart's voice drifted in, then faded out.

"Cloudy weather cloudy."

It was Earhart! Bellarts sent for Commander Thompson, who made his way to the radio room, half out of breath. What else? Was there any more? Nothing—that was all that could be discerned. But it was Earhart.

The minutes passed agonizingly, and heavy smoke began to collect in the radio room as ashtrays overflowed and men paced back and forth. Bellarts never took his hand from his ear and earphones for fear that he would miss her next transmission.

"*Itasca* from Earhart."

She was back! It was 2:48 A.M.

"*Itasca* broadcast on 3105 kilocycles on hour and half hour—repeat—broadcast on 3105 kilocycles on hour and half hour. Overcast."

Her voice came through weak, and she sounded far away. Bellarts strained to hear her. Leaning into his radio, he started to transmit by Morse code, not realizing she couldn't understand. "What is your position? When do you expect to arrive at Howland?"

Then he spoke into the mike: "What is your position? When do you expect to arrive at Howland?"

Silence. At all distances beyond 200 miles, voice signals on 3105 kilocycles would have ranged from weak to unreadable. There was nothing anyone could do but wait.

Questions were asked that no one could answer. Why didn't she respond? Were there problems with her radios?

An hour and five minutes later, more voice signals were received, but they were totally unreadable, even with five men in the radio room straining to listen on headphones and speakers. They could barely make her out, and worse yet, she wouldn't respond to their transmissions.

Radioman Third Class William Galten sat upright as Amelia's voice crackled back over the speaker at 5:12 A.M. "Want bearings on 3105 kilocycles on hour. Will whistle in microphone. Take a bearing on 3105 kilocycles." After whistling for a few seconds, she continued, "About 200 miles out."

Galten responded, but again, received no reply.

On Howland, Frank Ciprianti, manning the experimental direction finder, heard her and desperately fiddled with dials and his DF antenna. Earhart wouldn't stay on long enough for him to get a bearing. His frustration was mingled with anger.

The latest weather report, grabbed hastily by Thompson, showed squalls and overcast ending 40 miles northwest of the *Itasca.* The Electra was right in the middle of it.

"Give me the weather! I've got to have the weather!"

Amelia's voice came through full of tension. Galten tried to reply with everything at hand but, as he later recalled, "She failed to tell us on what channel and whether voice or code. So I put a ruler across all my radio keys and sent the weather on every telegraph channel I had!" He then repeated it on all voice channels. No response.

The mood in the radio room had become almost morose. Commander Thompson had stopped pacing and slumped into a chair to listen. He sat and stared straight ahead.

She was back, a little clearer this time, at 5:45 A.M. She had been airborne for over 18 hours.

"Please take bearing on us and report in half hour. I will make noise in microphone. About 100 miles out. Position doubtful." For the next seven seconds she transmitted something.

The radiomen were completely beside themselves now. They

had to have at least two minutes to get any kind of bearing. What was she doing out there, anyway? The frequency she was using was close to impossible for getting a bearing. She was acting as if she knew nothing about radios.

Talking among themselves, Bellarts, Ciprianti and their assistants decided they would try to get Amelia to change frequencies. At 6:18 A.M. Bellarts broadcast, "Earhart from *Itasca*. Cannot take bearing on 3105 very good. Please send on 500 or do you wish to take a bearing on us? Go ahead, please."

There was no response.

They didn't know that the trailing antenna necessary for 500 kilocycles was lying on the ground back in the States.

As 7:30 A.M. slipped by, the men in the *Itasca*'s radio room were mesmerized by the soft hiss of radio static that seemed to tell the tale for most of the operation. It had been almost two hours since Earhart's last transmission. She was an hour overdue. What was she doing? Where was she?

Like an explosion, Amelia's voice burst loud and clear over the speakers at 7:42 A.M. at Howland. She had been flying for more than 20 hours.

"We must be on you but cannot see you but gas is running low. Have been unable to reach you by radio. We are flying at 1000 feet."

Can't see them? That smoke rising from the ship's funnel would have been visible for 30 miles! And she had not heard one transmission from the *Itasca*! Bellarts tried again and again to raise her.

Sixteen minutes later she was back with a very strong signal. "We are circling but cannot see the island. Cannot hear you. Go ahead on 7500 kilocycles with long count either now or on schedule time on half hour."

The tiny radio room was an arena of total confusion. No one had ever heard of a ship or airplane DF that would take a bearing on 7500 kilocycles, so far up the frequency band. Bellarts was frantic—what could he do that he hadn't already done?

Without hesitation he tapped out a rapid series of dot-dash Morse code homing signals in spite of the knowledge that she was not hearing anything they were transmitting.

Five minutes later Amelia was back, her voice high-pitched and strained. "We received your signals but unable to get minimum. Please take bearings on us and answer on 3105 kilocycles with voice." She followed with a long dash for five seconds.

Immediately Bellarts called Ciprianti on Howland. "Did you get a cut on her?"

Ciprianti had not been able to get a bearing on Amelia's brief transmission either. Besides that, the borrowed gun batteries that were powering his radio had run down during the night, and the radio was almost dead.

It appeared to all who had listened to her that Amelia had no idea how to use her radios. She was switching back and forth from one frequency to another in confusion. Was she ignoring all of the messages from the *Itasca* sent the previous week concerning emergency direction-finding and voice communications?

A tragic, grotesque comedy of errors, with Amelia at center stage, was going to keep the Electra and its crew from landing at Howland. She was close, damn close. She had to be. The transmission was S-5, or full strength.

At 8:44 A.M. Amelia radioed, "We are on the line of position 157–337. Will repeat this message on 6210 kilocycles. Wait. Listening on 6210. We are running north and south."

With that final transmission, the outside world heard the last from Amelia Earhart. She and Fred Noonan vanished into the Pacific Ocean.

Chapter 2

Lady Pilot

1897–1935

HER first airplane ride—with the yet-to-be-famous barn-stormer Frank Hawks—changed the course of Amelia Mary Earhart's life. Years later, after she had learned to fly, she became the most famous pilot in the world next to Charles Lindbergh.

Amelia was born on July 24, 1897, in Atchison, Kansas. At the age of ten she saw her first airplane while attending the Iowa State Fair in Des Moines, but she recalled that "it was a thing of rusty wire and wood and looked not at all interesting." According to her younger sister, Muriel, Amelia was an energetic, restless tomboy constantly in search of action and adventure. Aviation had not yet captured her.

Toward the end of World War I she cared for war wounded in Toronto as a nurse's aide at Spadina Military Hospital, confronting the waste of war first-hand. Though she was often present at war rallies, the twenty-year-old became disillusioned with the magnitude of the killing. Pacifism became an integral part of Amelia's beliefs.

While in Toronto Amelia suffered the first of several periods of ill health during times of stress. In *Letters from Amelia*, her biographer, Jean L. Backus, notes that Amelia was plagued with severe sinus infections and congestion. This, to a pilot, would be somewhat akin to a sailor being cursed with sieges of acute sea-sickness. Any change in altitude while flying could cause severe pain from rapid increases or decreases in atmospheric pressure. Backus points out that "her body responded to sights and sounds and smells of distress in others with pain and pressure around one eye and copious drainage via the nostrils and throat." This torment persisted throughout her life, particularly after her solo flights in 1932 and 1935. But "Amelia had learned early that one never complained of or ever admitted anything adverse or disagreeable about oneself or a family member."

As World War I ended, aviation once again entered Amelia's life. She was visiting an exposition in Toronto when a group of military pilots just returned from the war put on a display of their skills. These "heroes of the hour," as she remembered them in *Last Flight*, put their aircraft through a series of impressive aerobatics. Amelia and one of her friends sat in the middle of a clearing to watch the show. One of the pilots decided to see if he could make the two girls scatter by diving down at them. Her friend fled in terror, but Amelia stared in fascination, feeling "mingled fear and pleasure which surged over me as I watched that small plane at the top of its earthward swoop. Commonsense told me if something went wrong with the mechanism, or if the pilot lost control, he, the airplane and I would be rolled up in a ball together. I did not understand it at the time but I believe that little red airplane said something to me as it swished by." Though Earhart was then studying for a career in medicine, she could not forget airplanes from that moment on.

During her 1920 summer vacation, in California, she attended every air meet she could find and finally got the chance to ride in an airplane with Frank Hawks, later recalling that "by the time I had got two or three hundred feet off the ground I knew I had to fly." Her initial flight training was with Anita "Neta" Snook, the first woman graduate of the Curtiss School of Aviation. With the help of her adventurous mother, Amy Otis Earhart, and against the wishes of her father, Edwin, she bought a used, bright yellow Kinner Canary on her twenty-fifth birthday, July 24, 1922.

Amelia continued to fly for fun. After spending a semester in 1924 as a pre-med student at Columbia University in New York, she dropped out and took a job teaching English to foreign students in Boston. The next year she turned to social work at Denison House, first part-time, then full-time, at a salary of sixty dollars a month. Amelia's instincts for helping others were deepseated. Not only had she seen the suffering of the wounded she had cared for ten years earlier, but she had watched her father battle alcoholism during her childhood.

When Edwin Earhart became an alcoholic, his wife and two daughters held the family together on the exterior so that friends and neighbors would not realize he had suffered more than a "general nervous breakdown." Instead of trying to deal with the problem openly, Amelia learned to take up any slack through sheer force of will and became overly protective of her mother and younger sister while never coming to grips with "Dad's sickness." Finally the strain of Edwin's habit on the family was more than her mother could cope with, and although Amelia wanted harmony, her parents could never reconcile their differences and they eventually divorced. When Edwin died a few years later, in 1930, Amelia saw him as aristocratic to the end in spite of his debilitating habit. Living in something of a fantasy world with regard to her father, she never lost faith in him and paid all of his bills regardless of the problems he caused. This unrealistic view of alcoholism would cause her to trust Wilmer Stultz in 1928 and Fred Noonan in 1937, even though they both should have been removed from their duties because of their inability to stay off the bottle on the job.

Amelia felt she should have done more to help her father overcome his problem. As Jean Backus noted, Amelia thought and acted "for the good of those who might not think and act correctly for themselves. If this made her seem arrogant and patronizing to others, either she did not realize it or did not care." Her strong will, in her own mind, was for the benefit of those she could help. If that upset a few, they would have to take it like medicine. Until her disappearance, Amelia would have a firm hand in her family's affairs, particularly those of her mother and sister.

In May 1928, Amelia Earhart's life was changed forever by a phone call from publishing heir George Palmer Putnam. He had been charged by Mrs. Frederick (Amy) Guest to choose the first woman to fly the Atlantic, as a passenger in the Fokker trimotor *Friendship* she had purchased from Commander Richard E. Byrd. Amelia's quick reply, a simple yes, propelled her into another world.

Her first meeting with Putnam in New York was a disaster as far as Amelia was concerned. Even though she had acceptable credentials as a student pilot, she thought she had left this important man unimpressed. She later told her friend Marion Perkins that he was "a fascinating man. . . . Once he got me to the station [in a taxi], he hustled me aboard the Boston train like a sack of potatoes. Didn't offer to pay my fare back home either!" This was a display of the unbounded energy that Putnam possessed. As Amy Guest's promoter, Putnam wanted a flying heroine to match Lindbergh, even though the woman chosen to fly the Atlantic on the float-equipped Fokker would be only a passenger. The public's impression was the important thing. A few days after meeting Putnam, Amelia was chosen.

With Commander Byrd as technical consultant, pilot Wilmer L. "Bill" Stultz and mechanic Louis "Slim" Gordon prepared the Fokker for the voyage. In aviation circles, there were few men more qualified to get the *Friendship* safely across the Atlantic. Amelia went back to Denison House to continue her work, taking a few breaks to watch the preparations, which were hidden from the press. What the outside world saw was Richard Byrd getting the *Friendship* ready for a flight to the South Pole.

On June 3, 1928, the Fokker, carrying Earhart, Stultz and Gordon, left Boston Harbor on the initial leg of the flight, to Halifax. The *Christian Science Monitor* was the first to release the real story, with a photo of Amelia bearing the caption "She Has the Lindbergh Look." Much to her disgust, the resemblance and similar public personality would forever brand her "Lady Lindy."

By June 5 the trimotor was moored at Trepassey, Newfoundland, for the over-ocean leg, but weather delayed the trio for a discouraging thirteen days. As boredom and frustration set in, Bill Stultz found it increasingly difficult to resist his one weakness, alcohol. Both Amelia and Slim were doubtful Stultz would be sober enough to fly when the weather finally cleared. She later told GP, as she nicknamed Putnam in accordance with her own preference for being called "AE," that the time spent at Trepassey "taxed her spirit more than any experience she'd ever faced."

Amelia was again confronted with the problem that had plagued her father, and she responded in the same way, by bearing the burden. She had tried to keep her family together through force of will, and she would now do the same thing to assure the success of the flight.

When Slim Gordon threatened to call it quits if Earhart, who had been placed in charge of the flight, didn't send for backup pilot Lou Gower, Amelia almost gave in, but as Putnam recounted in his book *Soaring Wings*, "AE was a scrupulously fair person, and she knew that she could not do that without great damage to Stultz. . . . She'd started something, and she would go through with it. Granting that he was in proper shape, she knew that Stultz could fly the Friendship as no one else could. Very well. She'd make it her job to keep him—for as much as she could—in proper shape, so that when the time came to embark he'd be ready."

Amelia took seriously her position as captain of the flight. Recalling how she had tried to help her father in times of stress, she enlisted Slim in getting Bill away from the bottle. They dragged him out for walks on the beach—anything to get him out of his room, where he would sit alone and drink. Apparently AE's confidence rubbed off on Slim. He decided to stick it out and make the flight.

On June 17 James H. "Doc" Kimball of the U.S. Weather Bureau in New York telegraphed word of fair skies over the North Atlantic for the next forty-eight hours. Searching out Stultz, Amelia found him so drunk he could not rise from his bed under his own power. Putnam later recalled that "AE did what I suppose either was the bravest or the silliest act of her whole career. . . . She simply got hold of her pilot and all but dragged him to the plane. It was a fine-drawn choice. He wasn't in good shape, but perhaps—once he took off—his flying instinct, which was so sure, so complete, would come uppermost."

After Slim helped her get Bill into the cockpit, Amelia found that her pilot had left nothing to chance. A bottle had been carefully hidden in the cabin. Knowing the courage that an alcoholic drew from the presence of a bottle, she decided to ignore her instinct to throw it out the trap door. What if Bill found it missing and then fell apart? Wouldn't the comfort of knowing it was there carry him through? "There might come a moment," Putnam related, "when, to keep going, he *must* have the contents of that bottle." The contraband cargo stayed aboard.

Stultz recovered enough to get the *Friendship* started, but his skills seemed to wane there. He gunned the engines and taxied downwind at increasing speed, rocking and staggering the aircraft with very little finesse. Heading the Fokker into the wind, he applied full throttle and lurched off, with the engines coughing and sputtering as they gulped saltwater spray shot up from the bouncing floats. Stultz aborted the run after failing to reach the required 50 mph for liftoff, then abandoned two more takeoff attempts. Finally, on the fourth try, Bill summoned the skill to reach 50 mph on the airspeed indicator, in spite of the two outboard engines "coughing salt water." They were on their way at 9:15 A.M.

As the aircraft started to cruise across the Atlantic, Stultz drew strength from being in his element. From that point on he skillfully piloted the *Friendship* on course, never taking a drink. AE finally threw the bottle into the Irish Sea.

Amelia stayed at the chart table and filled in the logbook while Bill and Slim did the flying and navigating; she was happy just to be a part of the adventure. After 20 hours and 40 minutes Stultz made an excellent landing at Burry Port, Wales, on the morning of June 18. The first woman had crossed the Atlantic by air.

Amelia was looking forward to slipping back into anonymity, for she did not actually pilot the aircraft. The pilot and the navigator deserved the credit, not the passenger. After sensational receptions in Southampton and London, however, it became clear that Amelia Earhart would forever be in the public spotlight. As she remembered in *Last Flight,* "After the pleasant accident of being the first woman to cross the Atlantic by air, I was launched into a life full of interest. Aviation offered such fun as crossing the continent in planes large and small, trying the whirling rotors of an autogiro, making record flights. With these activities came opportunity to know women everywhere who shared my conviction that there is so much women can do in the modern world and should be permitted to do irrespective of their sex. Probably my greatest satisfaction was to indicate by example now and then, that women can sometimes do things themselves if given the chance."

But there were drawbacks as well. Being thrust into the public eye, with her privacy gone, Amelia "really didn't feel safe anywhere, and she had to put on an outside," according to her mother. The dispassionate, calm, cool aviatrix wore a mask that became a part of her public personality. However, according to those close to her, she did not really believe the growing legend that surrounded her.

Before leaving England, Amelia managed to make an enjoyable two-hour flight in Lady Mary Heath's Avro Avian Moth biplane. Over the ocean she had been forced to watch as others did the flying. In the Moth she handled the controls herself, reaffirming her own worth as an aviator. Before she sailed for New York on the *President Roosevelt,* AE purchased the Avian, with the idea of crossing the American continent in it. During the cruise home, ship's captain Harry Manning gave his now-famous passenger some instruction in celestial navigation, but she found its complexities somewhat boring. Bill Stultz got drunk, staying secluded for most of the cruise. Though Amelia tried to help, she finally gave up. She was not up to working with Bill again.

Back in America, she went off on a publicity tour arranged by Putnam. She did not yet realize that this would become a way of life for her, a life she often found difficult to tolerate, since it removed her from flying for long periods. As he had done with Lindbergh and his book *We,* Putnam arranged for Amelia to write a book on the flight for his company, G. P. Putnam's Sons, entitled *20 Hrs. 40 Min.* He offered Amelia the use of his Rye, New York, estate after the tour so she could have the privacy she needed. Then he told her he would be her unofficial manager and adviser on commercial endorsements and her new writing career. Apparently Amelia accepted the arrangement without protest. She spent a great deal of time with Putnam and his wife, Dorothy, and found their friendship satisfying enough to dedicate the book to Dorothy.

In September the manuscript of *20 Hrs. 40 Min.* was completed and sent to the publisher just as the Moth biplane arrived from England. Eager to be in the air, away from the pressures of being well known, Amelia went to Los Angeles, where she attended the National Air Races.

Shortly thereafter Putnam sent Amelia on her first lecture tour. According to Jean Backus, "from now on, almost without exception, fall, winter and spring would be devoted to one-night stands on the circuit. Universities, colleges, men's clubs, women's clubs, civic forums, everyone wanted to hear Amelia Earhart speak." She was also committed to eight articles a year on aviation as an associate editor of *Cosmopolitan.* However, the lectures were the most demanding. A typical schedule would require her to make twenty-seven engagements in a single month with barely enough time to get from one to the next. By the beginning of 1929 AE was also traveling for Transcontinental Air Transport, founded by Eugene Vidal, who became one of her close friends, and Paul Collins. The airline's technical committee chairman was Charles Lindbergh.

Putnam presented Amelia to the public as an accomplished aviatrix, but in many cases she found herself having to rely on the abilities of others when flying unfamiliar aircraft. Elinor Smith, a teenager who was breaking a number of aviation records, found herself very much liking the private Amelia Earhart. The major obstacle in their relationship was Putnam's ruthlessness in promoting Amelia. In Elinor's case, this took the form of threatening her with banishment from the aviation scene unless she agreed, for the princely sum of $75 a week, to anonymously fly Amelia around the United States on an upcoming speaking tour. She would be identified only as Amelia's mechanic; she would have to avoid personal interviews and make sure that she was never photographed standing to Amelia's right (this was to forestall any copywriter from putting her name ahead of Amelia Earhart's in a picture caption). According to Elinor and other contemporaries, Amelia knew little of these underhanded efforts. Elinor felt that as much as Amelia wanted to fly, she was not getting enough time at the stick because of GP's hectic publicity schedule.

In her book *Aviatrix* Smith remembered flying with AE at the Bellanca factory in New Castle, Delaware.

> George Haldeman invited her to go up for a trial spin, and the three of us took off. She sat up front with him, and I stayed down in the last of the cabin's six seats. We had climbed to about 1,000 feet when George leveled off and motioned to Amelia to take over the controls. Our big, calm bird suddenly lurched out of control and wobbled all over the sky. Amelia was embarrassed and motioned George to take over. He landed, and we disembarked in silence.
>
> She pulled me aside and asked if we could go up again by our-

selves. . . . When I had climbed to 2,000 feet, I guided Amelia through some gentle, banking turns, carefully explaining the ship's normal flight position. . . . Again we slipped and skidded all over the sky. I was baffled, for once the ship's flying position was established, the rest of it should have been exactly like flying a small biplane. . . . I set down at the far end of the field to give her time to compose herself and me time to think of something to say. I have yet to live through a more awkward moment. Either Lady Lindy had never flown at all, or she had flown only briefly and quite some time ago. Today's performance didn't make any sense, except for Lady Heath's speculations that it was always Earhart's copilots (or "mechanics," as Putnam called them) who had done her flying.

In August 1929, Amelia entered the first Women's Air Derby, a race from California to Cleveland, flying a fast Lockheed Vega purchased with part of the proceeds from the sale of her Moth. This "Powder Puff Derby," as the event became known, was an opportunity for women pilots to display their skills. After a series of harrowing experiences, including the death of Marvel Crosson, the nine-day race was over. Louise Thaden came in first.

Elinor Smith watched as Amelia

finished a full two hours behind Louise, a disappointing third. Because she was flying the fastest ship in the race, her lack of expertise in both navigation and flying was pitilessly exposed. Her landing in Cleveland was amateurish as she bounced the big monoplane completely across the vast airport. There were snide remarks from onlookers when she frantically braked the ship out of a ground loop before rolling to a stop. But at that moment I was filled with admiration for her. Had her detractors known what they were looking at, they would have been cheering.

It was barely five months since the New Castle incident. In that short time Amelia had obtained her private license (because of Putnam's careful statements, few were aware that she hadn't had this all along) and made the transition from solo student to racing competitor. There was absolutely no way she could have built up enough air time in that brief period to be at ease behind the controls of the fastest heavy monoplane in the air.

Though there has been controversy over the topic of just when AE obtained her pilot's license and how many hours she actually logged in the air, neither the license nor a logbook has been found. Her friend Louise Thaden said that Amelia had little feel for seat-of-the-pants flying. She was a by-the-book pilot who could operate the machinery quite well but found herself at a loss when an aircraft had to be handled with skill alone.

Shortly after the race some women pilots banded together to form their own organization, the Ninety-Nines, named after the number of charter members. This knot of aviation enthusiasts not only would prove to be crucial in getting more women to take to the air but would serve to enhance the public's awareness that flying was for everyone.

In less than a year after the *Friendship*'s crossing, GP had made himself a part of AE's life, much to the consternation of the newspaper reporters who followed her career. As Backus noted, "A tall lean man, full of impatient energy, his talent lay in propelling others to the celebrity status he never managed for himself, a source of personal displeasure that showed when he thrust himself into every conversation, every interview, every photograph he possibly could. Reporters complained later that to get a few words from Amelia they had to listen to hundreds from him."

By the end of 1929 Putnam had divorced Dorothy and made the first of six marriage proposals to Amelia, who kept turning him down. AE's steady suitor, Sam Chapman, a chemical engineer who had been a boarder at her parents' home in Los Angeles, had pursued her for years but would not share her with aviation—it had to be him or flying. Amelia could not bind herself to anyone who was not willing to let her continue flying whenever and wherever she wished. But this did not stop her from seeing Chapman, in spite of Putnam's regular proposals. Louise and Herb Thaden would often meet with Amelia for secret airborne double dates with Amelia and Sam. Yet as strongly as she felt for Sam, Amelia could not leave flying for him. She had no desire to see her horizons limited.

In spite of GP's hoopla, Amelia knew her limitations. She had been elected first president of the Ninety-Nines, with Louise Thaden as secretary, and was more determined than ever to advance the cause of women in aviation. Suggestions of a solo flight across the Atlantic Ocean were made by friends, but she replied to one, "I admit I should like to do it, but I know it would be fool-hardy for me to attempt it until I've had considerably more flying and navigation experience. Give me say, eighteen months to two years and then we'll see."

When her father, Edwin, died of stomach cancer in September 1930, AE foundered emotionally, suffering another period of illness due to stress. Realizing she had no stable home, she found loneliness a very real problem. Her mother, Amy, was not able to provide companionable support, needing to divide her time between a terminally ill sister and Amelia's sister, Muriel.

In spite of AE's unconventional attitudes toward settling down, Putnam's persistence started to pay off, perhaps because of the trauma she had faced with the death of her father and her separation from her mother. GP offered the only opportunity of having a home and a career at the same time. And even if he had remained just her business manager, they would have continued to be closely involved on all levels.

Wanting to make the right decision, Amelia turned to only two people for advice on marrying George Putnam. Carl "C.B." Allen of the New York *World* and Lauren P. "Deke" Lyman of the New York *Times* were two of the most respected aviation writers in the world. They knew Amelia and many of her fellow aviators. Both were known for truth in reporting rather than sensationalism. Consequently, they found themselves party to many confidences that never appeared in their columns. The morning that C.B. received a frantic call from Amelia, asking that he and Deke meet with her, stood out in his mind the rest of his life.

When the two arrived at Earhart's New York hotel suite, she told them, "It's about Mr. Putnam and me." Explaining that she had denied the marriage rumors because she was not ready to consider such an arrangement, she admitted, "I guess I squelched Gippy about as firmly as the report; he sulked about it awhile but he has subsequently apologized—and he still wants to marry me.

"Both of you have been good friends to me ever since we first met. I admire and trust you and I asked you to come over here because I want your honest opinion on whether I should marry this man who has done so much to guide and advance my flying career during the past three years. I owe him a lot and would like to repay him in some way for his help and kindness. But I am uncertain that marrying him would, in anywise, do that. Please tell me what you really think about it."

C.B. and Deke stared at her, finding it difficult to believe what she was saying. C.B. told her that Putnam was obviously able to get into the grubby business of exploiting her career to maximum benefit, something AE, with her high ideals, would find hard to do. "It may be that you need him as much or more than he needs you," he went on, but both men ended the session by saying the final decision would have to be hers alone. Amelia thanked them and said, "I've got to do some more soul-searching but your coming over has helped a lot."

Late in the fall of 1930, at the Lockheed factory in Burbank, California, GP asked Amelia for the sixth time to marry him. She casually accepted.

In a letter to her mother written on February 4, 1931, she gave no word of the coming marriage. She told of being due in Washington that night after a luncheon in Newark the same day, noting, "I shant be home over this next weekend. Why don't you plan your and girls trip for next one. Of course if you wish, come anyway." She made no further mention of coming events. Amelia and George were married three days later, on February 7. Her mother let it be known later that she had been against the union from the beginning: Putnam was twelve years older and divorced.

The now famous note written by AE and handed to GP on the morning of the wedding was frank and somewhat impersonal in allowing both partners to dissolve the marriage if, after a year, they found no happiness together.

> You must know again my reluctances to marry, my feeling that I shatter thereby chances in work which means so much to me. I feel the move just now as foolish as anything I could do. I know there may be compensations, but have no heart to look ahead.
>
> In our life together I shall not hold you to any medieval code of faithfulness to me, nor shall I consider myself bound to you similarly. . . . I cannot guarantee to endure at all times the confinements of even an attractive cage.

Thirteen-year-old Robert Anderson, the son of Judge Arthur Anderson, who performed the ceremony in the house the Putnam family owned in Noank, Connecticut, sat down with Amelia on a small couch just before the wedding took place. They struck up a conversation centering around aviation and the military applications of the autogyro in particular. Both the Army and the Navy were interested in the machine, but Anderson recalled Earhart mentioning that the Army apparently was not serious.

As the wedding party rose, Amelia was in the middle of her discourse. She quickly broke away, went through the five-minute ceremony, returned to the sofa and, Anderson remembered, "sat down and looked up at me. She said the Navy had made more progress in its tests with the autogyro." Judge Anderson came over and wished her every happiness, calling AE "Mrs. Putnam." Amelia corrected him, "without hospitality," according to Anderson, saying she would continue to use her maiden name in her work.

AE's friends believed that George was not in love with Amelia, nor she deeply in love with him. The arrangement was one that cemented their future partnership in aviation. She wanted to fly; he wanted to promote her as the best flier in the world. Throughout their six years of marriage they worked together, but each had times to pull apart to be alone. GP had once said that "AE was a 'loner' at heart," something he accepted.

The wedding remained a minor event in AE's life compared to her involvement in aviation. During early 1931 she had the opportunity to check out in a Pitcairn autogyro. This predecessor of the helicopter proved to be a hard machine to handle, Earhart not knowing "whether I flew it, or it flew me." On April 8 she made two flights over Willow Grove, Pennsylvania. During the last attempt she coaxed the autogyro to 18,415 feet, a record for rotor-winged aircraft, attracting the attention of the Beech-Nut Packing Corporation, which wanted her to make a cross-country flight in the Pitcairn to advertise their products.

The flight out to Oakland, California, was problem-free, but on the way back she crashed on takeoff at Abilene, Texas. A letter of reprimand was sent to AE from the Department of Commerce. Some newspapers reported she was "careless and used bad judgment," but in *Soaring Wings* Putnam reported that Amelia later said, "We'd have made it but for the crowd. The air just went out from under me at 30 or 50 feet up—maybe one of those hot little whirlwinds did it. We might have made it anyway, but I was afraid a child might run out suddenly or we might hit a car. Both crowds and automobiles were parked too closely infield. I did what I thought was best in the circumstances." She arrived back in Newark on June 22, 1931, after 11,000 miles and 150 hours' flying time.

Amelia continued to fly the autogyro. On September 17, with GP waiting in the crowd, Amelia again wrecked the Pitcairn, while landing at Detroit. She wrote Amy about the crash, saying, "My giro spill was a freak accident. The landing gear gave way from a defect and I ground-looped only. The rotors were smashed as usual with giros, but there wasn't even a jar. GP fell over a wire running to pick me up." Others who saw the accident said AE's rate of descent had been too fast and she had simply landed too hard, collapsing the landing gear.

More money than ever now came in from Earhart's speaking engagements and promotional endorsements, all arranged by Putnam. GP dreamed up and then handled a number of projects centered around the AE legend and name. These included the still famous Amelia Earhart luggage, women's sports clothes, lounging pajamas and tailored suits, Amelia Earhart Time Savers stationery, along with favorable comments for car engines, spark plugs, gasoline and everything connected with the aircraft she flew.

As her financial burdens decreased, Amelia tried to improve the lives of her mother and sister. No doubt she had good intentions, but she was often domineering, seeing herself as the head of the family now that Edwin was gone. She resented Muriel's problems with her husband, Albert Morrissey, who showed little desire to provide for his family. This was exactly the situation that proved her point on how antiquated marriage was and how it dragged women down from their true potential.

Money sent to Amy would often end up with Muriel, but Amelia did not like her mother to pass on her personal gifts. It was not that AE failed to help her sister substantially. She made $2500 available to the Morrisseys so they could buy their house, but her request for a formal loan agreement to be signed in a businesslike manner irritated the family. Muriel never complied with the requirement.

Whenever AE wanted to see Amy, she seemed to be tied up

with the Morrissey household. Mrs. Earhart later recalled, "We neither of us had much time for confidential talks because of schedules and things. It was utterly impossible and I reached a stage where I felt the only time I had a chance to talk to her was when I was holding on to her coat tails."

Though Amelia never intended to alienate her family, it was in some ways inevitable since she was so radically different in her lifestyle from her more conservative relatives. Jean Backus mused, "There is no doubt that Amelia loved both her mother and sister, but one wonders if she ever understood either woman; if she, who could happily exist by herself, ever acknowledged the need of most people *not* to be solitary."

By early 1932 Amelia was suffering under the pressure of the image her husband had created. She confided to some of her friends in the Ninety-Nines that she felt a fraud at times because of her lack of experience. There was little doubt that she was sincere in wanting to promote the cause of women in aviation, but there was not much regard for her ability as a pilot and she knew it. It was time to make a true record flight.

She sold her first Lockheed Vega and bought a newer version, resplendent in red and gold paint. She felt confident enough in it to attempt greater things. One morning at breakfast in Rye, she asked GP, "Would you *mind* if I flew the Atlantic?" By early April the pioneer arctic aviator Bernt Balchen was her technical consultant. He leased the Vega for a supposed South Pole flight with Lincoln Ellsworth that did not involve Earhart, a way to avoid publicity. Putnam wanted to downplay the involvement of others in the attempt, so that when the time came all attention would be focused on Amelia. Before long the sleek monoplane was at Teterboro Airport in New Jersey, under the hands of Lockheed mechanic Eddie Gorski, for reconditioning.

Once the aircraft was ready for the transatlantic attempt, only good weather was needed for departure. On May 20, 1932, Doc Kimball's forecast was favorable, and the Vega left for St. John's, Newfoundland, with Balchen at the controls and Amelia and Gorski aboard. The next day they flew to Harbour Grace. Amelia opted to lie down near the extra fuel tank to rest up for the evening departure. As Balchen and Gorski made final adjustments to the new Pratt & Whitney engine, the fuel system and other items, Amelia napped.

At 7:12 P.M. Amelia took off alone for Europe. Though the first portion of the flight was through wonderfully clear weather, that did not last for long. Her recollections of that night were of

> seeing . . . the flames lick through the exhaust collector ring and wondering, in a detached way, whether one would prefer drowning to incineration. Of the five hours of storm, during black midnight, when I kept right side up by instruments alone, buffeted about as I never was before. Of much beside, not the least the feeling of fine loneliness and of realization that the machine I rode was doing its best and required from me the best I had. . . .
>
> I carried a barograph. . . . At one point it recorded an almost vertical drop of three thousand feet. It started at an altitude of something over 3000 feet, and ended—well, something above the water. That happened when the plane suddenly "iced up" and went into a spin. How long we spun I do not know. I do know that I tried my best to do exactly what one should do with a spinning plane, and regained flying control as the warmth of the lower altitude melted the ice. As we righted and held level again, through the blackness below I could see the white-caps too close for comfort.

With daylight and transfer to the auxiliary fuel tank, AE discovered a fuel leak. A Paris landing was abandoned in favor of heading northeast for Ireland. A northwest wind had made her think she was south of her course, but later she said she had probably been right on it. Seeing the Irish coast, she dropped down along the Donegal hills under thunderstorms and followed a rail line, hoping it would lead to an airport. Nothing. There were plenty of cow pastures, however, so after 15 hours and 39 minutes she landed in a meadow near Londonderry on a Saturday afternoon, May 21, exactly five years after Charles Lindbergh had arrived in Paris. To Earhart's disgust and Putnam's delight, the Lady Lindy legend and nickname now became a part of the world's consciousness.

After Amelia was reunited with GP in England, they took a quick tour across Europe and then headed back for the United States, where the National Geographic Society awarded her its special gold medal. Only eight pilots had received it before her. Putnam wasted no time in getting Amelia back before the public with a series of appearances and lectures. Many observers were awed at her stamina—not for crossing the Atlantic, but for tirelessly keeping several engagements a day.

In the process of getting around the country in 1932, AE set a women's transcontinental speed record by flying nonstop from Los Angeles to Newark on August 24–25 in 19 hours and 5 minutes. This not only kept her name before the public but allowed her to do that which pleased her most, fly.

The next year Amelia entered the Bendix transcontinental race, sharing cockpit duties with Ruth Nichols, to compete for the special women's prize of $2500. The four male competitors would divide the major prize of $9000 with a $1000 bonus if the westbound record was broken. AE took off for Los Angeles in her red Vega on July 1, 1933, and came in third among all the competitors and ahead of the only other woman participant, Ruth Nichols. Then on July 7–8 she broke her own record of the year before by flying back to Newark in 17 hours and 7½ minutes.

Amelia first considered flying the Pacific solo after six U.S. Navy aircraft made the crossing from California to Hawaii in January 1934, but her heavy lecture schedule precluded any serious preparations for at least the balance of the year. By fall she told GP that she wanted to make the flight soon, flying from Honolulu to San Francisco because "it's easier to hit a continent than an island."

Christmas day 1934 was spent aboard the Matson liner SS *Lurline* bound for Honolulu with Amelia's faithful Vega NR965Y lashed to the aft tennis deck. With the Putnams were technical adviser Paul Mantz and his wife, Myrtle. The first woman to fly the Atlantic was on her way to try to become the first woman to fly the Pacific.

Mantz had come up the hard way, earning his reputation as a movie, stunt and charter pilot with a combination of skill and careful preparation. Unlike so many of the barnstorming pilots of the 1920s and 1930s, Mantz never did anything without first planning it out in great detail, so that what others might have thought foolhardy, he knew was possible within the limits of man and machine.

Just before the New Year, the Vega was unloaded and taken to the Army's Wheeler Field. Mantz began airborne tests of the engine and the fuel system, as well as the radio. There was mounting criticism of the flight, after several aircraft were lost trying to make it from the mainland to Hawaii. Rumors spread that the flight would be extremely dangerous because the radios had a range of only 300 miles. Mantz climbed the Lockheed to 12,000 feet over Diamond Head and talked to KFI, a commercial station in Los Angeles, 2570 miles away. Mantz had little doubt he would be able to get through; Walter McMenamy, an amateur radio operator and a part of the Mantz team, had helped KFI's engineers align their receiving equipment. In addition, other stations as far away as 3000 miles heard him quite clearly and answered. Paul's firm belief in adequate radios was something he never tired of emphasizing.

Criticism was also focused on AE for trying for the $10,000 prize offered by a group of businessmen, including sugarcane and pineapple growers. Some felt that she had sold out to the sugar interest by serving as a flying endorsement for them as they lobbied for pending legislation in Congress to reduce the sugar tariff. GP noticed that this criticism weighed heavily on Amelia, whose ideals were always high, even if his motives were more mercenary. When the sponsors of the prize told her they were thinking of withdrawing support, she shot back that they were cowards, afraid of public opinion. She would make the flight whether they sponsored her or not. The backing remained.

Inclement weather was the last hurdle. Torrential rain lasted for several days, until, on the afternoon of January 11, 1935, it lessened enough for Amelia to slip out alone on what was announced to be a test flight. At 4:44 P.M. she shoved the throttle forward, and the plane began to waddle through the mud, which flew in a wake behind the propeller. As Amelia glanced down the runway toward the normally sharp mountain ridges, all she saw were low gray clouds obscuring the peaks. Looking over at the flags lining the runway, she realized she was actually taking off downwind, but after using only 2000 feet of the 6000-foot runway, a bump threw the Vega into the air. Though the Lockheed almost settled back onto the mud runway, it slowly gained speed and AE was off.

After passing Makapuu Point at 6000 feet, the last bit of land before California, Amelia manually cranked out her trailing antenna, a chore she always detested, and sent her first message. In those days an antenna of this type was absolutely essential for proper radio communication. Mantz would no more have considered making long-distance flights without this equipment than without a good engine. Amelia and GP had a more casual attitude toward radios, but Mantz had made sure the gear was aboard.

That first message was heard by Putnam at KGU in Honolulu, but it was full of engine noise. She recalled that when he asked AE to speak louder, it "was thrilling to have his voice come in so clear to me, sitting out there over the Pacific. It was really one of the high points of the flight." With voice communications this good, there seemed to be little reason for learning Morse code, although that was a far more reliable means of radio transmission and reception with the equipment available in the mid-1930s. Amelia never bothered to master a telegraph key, relying strictly on voice.

In contrast, other fliers saw the importance of using every possible radio aid. Anne Morrow Lindbergh, the wife of Charles Lindbergh, became a proficient radio operator during the couples' many world flights. During their South Atlantic crossing in 1933 she kept in contact with the Pan Am network at distances of over 4000 miles and stayed in regular Morse contact with Pan American operators up and down the Latin American coast. She became skilled in cranking the trailing antenna out a certain number of turns for each frequency—for example, 48 turns equaled 3130 kilocycles.

Amelia's flight that night was one of stars and moonlit clouds over a black sea. Nine hundred miles out, she was tuned in to KFI in Los Angeles and signaling to ships below. She held her compass course as carefully as she knew how, since there were no other means of navigating—she had no experience with celestial or radio navigation. By midnight the moon had gone down and the Vega penetrated several minor rain squalls. Alone with the stars, AE later philosophized, "I have often said that the lure of flying is the lure of beauty, and I need no other flight to convince me that the reason flyers fly, whether they know it or not, is the esthetic appeal of flying."

As the sun came up, Amelia was enthralled with its intensity and had to put on dark glasses. "In addition to enjoying its beauty, that dawn over the Pacific was disconcerting. For the sun made its appearance well to the right of the course I was following. It seemed to me I should be flying much more in its direction than I was. For a brief moment I wondered if all night long I had been headed for Alaska! I checked my charts and I checked my compass and everything seemed to be as it should—so I could only conclude that the sun was wrong and I was right!"

After sunup the radio receiver quickly lost its effectiveness because of changed atmospheric conditions, and AE was flying over an extensive cloud deck. Still she continued to broadcast periodically, knowing that people were listening for her. When the clouds began to break up, she found the Dollar liner *President Pierce*, which was coming straight out from San Francisco. "It was going in the right direction, too, and just where it should be, according to my chart. And so was I." The sun's "wrong" position and its navigational implications never seemed to cross Amelia's mind again.

Lining up with the wake of the ship, which coincided with her charted course, AE headed for California, 300 miles away, and made landfall on course at San Francisco Bay. Landing at Oakland, 2400 miles from her takeoff point, she became the first person, male or female, to fly solo across any part of the Pacific Ocean and the first to solo over both the Atlantic and Pacific. Over 10,000 people were there to help her share the triumph.

This flight guaranteed Amelia Earhart an enduring place in aviation. She was living the legend in truth and not simply in GP's press campaign. Her optimism about her capabilities rose. She had earned her place in the sky. This confidence was reflected in the comments of Sir Anthony Jenkinson on February 5, 1935, after he spent some time with AE only a week after her return to Los Angeles. "This evening I sat next to Amelia Earhart—so modest, so natural and so feminine. Somehow one expects ocean fliers to be grim, tight-lipped people, but Miss Earhart is gay, smiling and friendly. Clearly hers is a mental rather than a physical courage, giving effect, not to bulging muscles and a philosophy of reckless, senseless daring, but rather to abundant confidence, poise and a firm, purposeful character." This "abundant confidence" was now beginning to show AE that she could make it through even the most harrowing flights.

Jenkinson went on to recall,

> She brought along with her the chart she used for the flight. It was about 2½ feet long and 8 inches wide and divided up into little sections, each of which represented one hour's flying. In each section—before the flight started—information and instructions relative to that particular hour's flying had been written. These instructions included the necessary alterations of the course to be made at the end of each hour.
>
> "You see," she said with a modest laugh, "the chart made navigation dead easy. All I had to do was to follow the written instructions at the end of every hour."

Certainly careful preparation and planning should have been a part of every flight, but for Amelia this kind of rigid, by-the-book approach was her only method of flying, as Louise Thaden had noticed many times. AE was able to follow a manual to the letter, but her flying instincts were not well honed. Those written instructions reflected the thoroughness of Paul Mantz, not Amelia Earhart, and being "off course" at sunrise was something AE found mystifying. Navigation and radio operation would never be her strong points.

By March Amelia "returned to N.Y. and found myself signed for the most strenuous lecture engagement ever undertaken." However, this in no way hindered her plans to accept an invitation from the president of Mexico to visit his country in her trusty Lockheed Vega. She plotted courses from Los Angeles to Mexico City to Newark which would result in more records.

To his dismay, Wiley Post unintentionally goaded her on. When AE told Post, whom she had known since his days as a test pilot at Lockheed, that she intended to go in a straight line on the last leg from Mexico to New York, he asked, "Are you cutting across the Gulf? That's about 700 miles. Almost half an Atlantic.

How much time do you lose if you go around by the shore?" AE replied that it was about an hour, and Wiley urged, "Amelia, don't do it. It's too dangerous."

"I couldn't believe my ears," she wrote later. "Did Wiley Post, the man who had braved every sort of hazard in his stratosphere flying, really regard a simple little flight from Mexico City to New York across the Gulf as too hazardous? If so, I could scarcely wait to be on my way." Amelia was now in her prime, confident she could do anything. She was ready to conquer new vistas with the assurance nothing would go wrong.

GP financed the flight by selling 780 autographed special stamped letter "covers," but stamp dealers around the world questioned the propriety of the effort, since there seemed to be doubt that all of the covers would be carried on the aircraft. Waiting in Mexico for Amelia, George issued a statement personally vouching for their authenticity.

On April 19, 1935, Amelia stopped by her dry cleaner's to pick up her flying suit and made her way to Burbank Airport, in Southern California's San Fernando Valley. Just before midnight she took off in 965Y with the letter covers aboard and headed into a beautiful moonlit sky. By the time she reached the Gulf of California, a white haze had settled in, making it hard to tell what was water and what was sand. A thousand miles out, below Mazatlán, her chart called for an easterly turn toward Mexico City, six hundred miles away. She made the course correction, thinking "I would escape the fate that had been promised me, that of straying on the final stretch of the journey."

When time came for her to arrive at her destination, however, there was no city in sight. To add to her problems, dirt or an insect irritated one of her eyes, and she had great difficulty reading her map through her pain and blurred vision. The combination of events made her decide to land and find out where she was. Upon landing on a dry lake bed among cacti, she was greeted by "cowboys and villagers [who] sprang up miraculously." Though neither side spoke the other's tongue, a map and sign language revealed Mexico City to be only fifty miles away. With her newfound friends holding back cattle, goats and children from the improvised runway, Amelia took off amidst great cheers and rejoicing. A half hour later she landed at Valbuena Field in Mexico

City after 13 hours and 32 minutes total time. George and the President of Mexico, Lázaro Cárdenas, were there to greet her.

She enjoyed the Mexican hospitality greatly, but fretted through eighteen days waiting for a good weather report from Doc Kimball. George had gone back to New York, and AE was anxious to get on with the next leg of the flight.

In order to have enough runway for a takeoff at 8000 feet above sea level, soldiers cleared a three-mile stretch on the Lake Texcoco mudflats and lined it with tiny flags. At last, shortly after midnight on May 8, Doc came up with a favorable report for the Gulf of Mexico, relayed by George on the phone to Amelia. By 6:06 A.M. Amelia was airborne after using only a mile of the runway.

Brushing over the mountains at 10,000 feet, Amelia headed for Tampico, then 700 miles out over the Gulf of Mexico for New Orleans. She gazed at the water. Thinking of Post's fears, she realized that she had flown over the Atlantic and Pacific mostly at night and over cloud cover. As she recalled,

> In the combined six thousand miles or more of previous over-ocean flying it happened I'd seen next to nothing of ocean.
>
> Given daylight and good visibility, the Gulf of Mexico looked large. And wet. One's imagination toyed with the thought of what would happen if the single engine of the Lockheed Vega should conk. Not that my faithful Wasp [engine] ever had failed me, or indeed, even protested mildly. But, at that, the very finest machinery *could* develop indigestion.
>
> So, on that sunny morning out of sight of land, I promised my lovely red Vega I'd fly her across no more water. And I promised myself that any further over-ocean flying would be attempted in a plane with more than one motor, capable of keeping aloft with a single engine. Just in case.
>
> Which, in a way, was for me the beginning of the world flight project. Where to find the tree on which costly airplanes grow, I did not know. But I did know the kind I wanted—an Electra Lockheed, big brother of my Vegas, with, of course, Wasp engines.

By the time Amelia Earhart arrived at Newark Airport, 2185 miles, and 14 hours and 19 minutes, after leaving Mexico, her distiny was set. She would fly around the world in Electra, the lost sister of Orestes.

Chapter 3

Around the World: The First Attempt

1935–1937

ONCE Amelia returned from Mexico, her husband wasted no time in placing her back on the lecture circuit. She was mobbed by the crowd when she landed at Newark on the evening of May 8, and friendly police officers nearly pulled her apart trying to keep the mass of humanity from tearing off her clothes. By the end of that month she had spoken in many cities, including Chicago, Washington, Atlanta, New York and Indianapolis.

In June 1935 Amelia joined Purdue University in Lafayette, Indiana, as a part-time lecturer and consultant to further the cause of getting women into aviation through the coeducational programs offered there. She had become a champion of women's rights: "I, for one, hope for the day when women will know no restrictions because of sex but will be individuals free to live their lives as men are free." AE considered Purdue a particularly forward-looking institution because it was building a respectable aviation department and was one of the few universities in the world with its own airfield.

The hectic pace brought another bout with the torture of sinusitis. As Amelia wrote her mother, she was "tired of being beaten up with washings out," so she entered Cedars of Lebanon Hospital in Los Angeles for surgery on June 25, the day after making a speech in Pasadena. Her body took some time to recover, and she was still running a fever ten days later, though her nasal passages were healing well. Exhaustion and illness, usually accompanied by periods of little rest and demanding schedules, were as much a part of Earhart's life as flying, perhaps more so.

While she was recuperating, the Vega was refurbished and

plans were made for getting back into the air. She entered the Los Angeles-to-Cleveland Bendix race in late August under the guidance of Paul Mantz. The only other woman to attempt the race was Jacqueline Cochran, who was flying a Northrop Gamma, vastly superior to the Vega. Mantz knew the other aircraft could beat Amelia's plane, but he estimated she could place fifth.

On August 31 the racers took off from California. As Mantz and his friend Al Menasco sat in the rear playing gin rummy, Amelia flew the Vega to Cleveland, coming in fifth, just as Mantz had said. Cochran had been forced to drop out of the race because of engine trouble, and AE went home with more experience and $500, enough to pay her expenses.

In September Amelia went into business with Mantz at United Air Services to start a flying school; made the Vega, along with Paul's, available for charter work; and even thought of forming an air circus. Though none of these schemes succeeded, Earhart and Mantz remained a solid team. This bothered Myrtle Mantz more than anyone suspected, and when she sued Paul for divorce in early 1936, she named Amelia as one of two corespondents, specifically as the "other woman" responsible for the breakup of the marriage.

For his part, Paul objected to "Gippy" Putnam's ruthless promotion of Amelia's career. The intense lecture schedule took its toll on her, not only running her down physically but robbing her of much-needed flight time. According to Putnam, AE "spoke 136 times in 1935 before audiences totaling 80,000." In 1936 she would speak 150 times.

During the last months of 1935 Amelia began to push harder to realize her dream of flying around the world. Mantz was involved from the beginning, bearing the burden of technical planning. More than anyone, he realized what a tremendous undertaking it would be to circumnavigate the globe at the equator. Amelia did not seem to understand how dangerous it could be, and Putnam talked about the kind of money that could be made, which irked Mantz greatly.

Putnam was determinedly lining up sponsorship and working hard behind the scenes to have Purdue serve as the gatherer of funds. In January 1936 GP wrote Paul, "It will follow a course unique in world flight attempts. That is, East to West ... San Francisco ... Hawaii ... Wake ... Manila ... and thence around the water course, the Red Sea and Mediterranean, and across the South Atlantic and up to Washington. For an Electra on floats to make the first round-the-world flight is a uniquely valuable exploitation bull's-eye!" Lockheed's new Electra, equipped with pontoons, was, in Mantz's view, the ideal aircraft in which to make the flight.

As if this letter did not irritate Mantz enough, GP wrote him another letter the same day, which was to be passed on to Lockheed. Putnam had approached Sikorsky about their S-43 flying boat, and quoted its price of $110,000 in an attempt to pressure Lockheed, but Mantz thought this was a bad way to do business.

On April 20, 1936, the president of Purdue, Edward C. Elliot, announced that a fund of $50,000 had been established by several members of the Purdue Research Foundation who wished to remain anonymous. The money would go into the new Amelia Earhart Fund for Aeronautical Research to purchase a Lockheed Electra without floats (less complex and expensive than a float-equipped plane), which, unknown to the public, had already been ordered on March 20. The sleek twin-engine transport would be turned over to AE for a number of airborne experiments. Several press releases were issued describing the aircraft as a flying laboratory to test such things as the effects of altitude on metabolism and fatigue brought on by instrument flying, but those were more attempts to conceal plans for the world flight from the public than anything else.

Reporters continually hounded AE about the possibility of a world flight, yet as late as May 22 she denied there were any plans for such a thing, saying, "That would take a year's preparation and might not even be feasible at all." In the meantime, Mantz began as tight a training regimen for AE as he could squeeze between her lecture tours. If she was going to survive a flight during which she would encounter some of the earth's worst weather, she would have to become a proficient instrument pilot. Many hours were spent in the Link blind-flying trainer in Burbank.

Since the Electra was basically a ten-passenger transport, Mantz set about redesigning the interior to make it an efficient long-distance machine. While he worked shooting movie scenes of Pan Am's new China Clipper, he studied the layout of the flying boat's chart room, navigation desk and cockpit, then set about scaling them down. He wrote Putnam, "A Sperry Robot Pilot is essential; it will eliminate fifty percent of her fatigue." After hard days of movie flying, Mantz spent many late nights trying to get the Electra just the way he wanted it.

By May 7 the Electra, though not completed internally, was ready for painting. Mantz wrote to GP, "I would suggest that the rudder, stabilizer, and a border on the top of the wing be painted orange or red, to be seen easier when the sky is overcast." Putnam did not like the idea, telling Mantz, "She'll want Purdue colors, gold and black." In the end, Mantz got what he wanted, and orange was the color chosen.

Of critical importance was the amount of fuel that could be carried aboard, particularly for the long and hazardous Pacific legs. Mantz contacted his old friend Clarence M. Belinn, superintendent of engineering for National Airways in Boston. This airline had experience flying Electras, which had nightmarish fuel-management problems.

Belinn devised a crossfeed system that Amelia could operate with one master valve on the floor of the cockpit, feeding gas from three tanks in each wing and six additional tanks in the fuselage, separating the cockpit and the navigator's station. A total of 1202 gallons could be carried, giving "her from 2500 to 3000 miles range, depending on winds and how she flew," Belinn recalled for Mantz's biographer Don Dwiggins.

Meanwhile GP was quietly obtaining political support for the trip. In early June he contacted Eleanor Roosevelt and asked her to get the State Department's help for the flight while maintaining strict confidentiality. The First Lady's secretary did the legwork and Richard Southgate, chief of the Division of Protocol, was assigned to handle the project, though discussions on the flight were deferred.

On July 22, 1936, Amelia flew Lockheed 10E NR16020 for the first time in Burbank with company test pilot Elmer C. McLeod.

The New York *Times* reported the plane's cost at $70,000, equipped with the latest in radios, Wasp engines of 1100 total horsepower, constant-speed propellers, and, optimistically, "enough fuel for 4500 miles nonstop."

Amelia was as delighted with the aircraft as Mantz was. This sleek, silver, very modern machine was as good as, if not better than, anything the military services were flying. Mantz, however, was presented with an entirely new challenge: Amelia had to learn how to handle this big twin-engine airplane. Training a single-engine pilot to cope with engine-out emergencies and crosswinds in a twin was hard enough without the student going off for weeks at a time to lecture and make public appearances. As Paul watched Amelia's progress, he noted that she would try to keep up with the plane's side-to-side motion by adjusting the throttles alternately to correct it; she could not seem to grasp how far a pilot could get "behind" when trying to control an aircraft with two engines, particularly on takeoff. He continually lectured her not to "jockey" the throttles, but rather to pull them back to idle and start over again when the aircraft yawed from side to side.

By late August Paul thought both plane and pilot were ready for a long shakedown, though there were still minor items that needed work. He secretly made preparations to have Amelia fly the Electra in that year's Bendix race. On August 30 Amelia, Paul and mechanic Bo McKneely flew to Kansas City from Burbank in 8 hours and 6 minutes. The press was on to them; questions flew about whether she was going to enter the Bendix in just a few days. By September 4 AE was entered in the race, this time from New York to Los Angeles, with Helen Richey, America's first female airline pilot, aboard as copilot. Trouble plagued them from the start. The aircraft's fuel lines didn't work properly. Halfway to California the navigation hatch, recently added, blew open. Fighting through to the end, Amelia again finished fifth. However, Louise Thaden and her copilot, Blanche Noyes, both AE's good friends, won the male-dominated event, much to AE's delight. The important thing in her eyes was for women to advance in aviation, though Putnam did not quite see it that way. He had a world flight to support.

The press continued to hound Amelia about rumors of the global attempt. Two weeks after the Bendix, she threw them a tempting morsel—"I'm nearly sold on this idea of flying around the world because I'd like to do it."

As September drew to a close, Putnam had not heard from the State Department. Prodded, Southgate told GP the government could not act officially to obtain foreign permissions until the flight had been approved by the Department of Commerce. Putnam wrote to that department on October 15, stating the "primary purpose of the flight is a thorough field test of this two-motored plane with its various items of modern scientific equipment." In describing the aircraft and its equipment, he said it would not carry firearms or photographic gear other than two small hand-held cameras.

Putnam described his surprising plans for the proposed route in detail. Flying from Oakland to Honolulu sounded possible, but to get to India, GP suggested going via either Manila or Tokyo (the only portions of the route that would not generally follow the equator). These legs were far beyond the capability of the Electra, since there were no plane facilities on land between Hawaii and either of the two cities.

Putnam thought the Pan Am Clipper flying boat base at Midway, though really not adequate for the Electra, could be used for aerial refueling. He asked Mantz why his Stearman biplane camera ship couldn't be used to haul gas up to Amelia as she went by. Mantz said it was possible, but all he could take up at one time was a hundred gallons, which would mean taking off and coming back to fill up five or six times. That would take over three hours, which made the plan ridiculous.

Nevertheless, GP wanted to try it. He wrote the Secretary of the Navy at the end of October asking for help in carrying off the attempt in the air over Midway. Putnam was confident that 500 gallons could be added to the 700 AE would still have aboard, giving her enough fuel to fly the 2800 miles to Tokyo or to Manila via Guam. He did not mention how she was to stay awake while flying 4000 miles nonstop.

Amelia apparently thought this plan could work; she wrote to President Roosevelt and asked his help in getting the Navy to cooperate. Her friendship with Eleanor would ensure the letter was read. She indicated her primary route would be as outlined, but she listed an alternate route from Honolulu to Brisbane, Australia. This seemed an even more unlikely route, since it covered 5000 miles without the possibility of aerial refueling, but it could be followed if the government prepared an airstrip at a tiny U.S. outpost, Howland Island, 1800 miles southwest of Hawaii. This new route seemed to make a great deal more sense, particularly since Howland, along with Jarvis Island, had been earmarked as the future site of an emergency runway. As of October 1936 no work had been done, but the next provisioning ship was due there in January.

At the end of November the Navy told the Putnams it would cooperate in refueling Amelia's plane over Midway if she would pay for the fuel and learn in-flight refueling techniques from a civilian, most likely Paul Mantz. Richard B. Black, Department of the Interior field representative in Honolulu, responsible for oversight of islands in the Pacific, had been refused approval for equipment to begin construction of the emergency field on Jarvis, not to mention Howland, leaving Earhart with the far-fetched scheme of aerial refueling if she was going to make it across the Pacific.

Black was determined, however. He radioed his superiors on December 2 that he had been able to coax the Army into lending him a tractor and a scraper. Robert L. Campbell, airport inspector for the Bureau of Air Commerce, had encouraged Black to seek further help by asking the Works Progress Administration to underwrite the work.

In the meantime, Putnam informed the State Department that "it had now been decided to change the route from the Hawaiian Island–Howland Island–Brisbane, Australia–Port Darwin, Australia" plan to an alternate route running from Howland Island to Port Moresby or Lae, New Guinea, and then to Port Darwin. A few days later, on December 7, apparently as a result of the Earhart/Putnam requests, Black was told the "proposed airplane landing field to be located Howland instead of Jarvis. [William T.] Miller [superintendent of airways, Bureau of Commerce] consulting Aubrey Williams, Works Progress Administration, and will propose that Howland landing field be designated WPA project."

As more people became aware of Earhart's desires, the lethargic American bureaucracy slowly responded. Eugene Vidal, director of the Bureau of Air Commerce and a good friend of the Putnams, radioed Robert Campbell on December 8 that he had seen Black's radiogram. He told Campbell to obtain more government equipment for the Howland project and go to the island on the next provisioning cruise to oversee the effort. Campbell was cautioned not to release any information on the project. Vidal told him in a letter that since Earhart was "including Howland as one of her stops, it enable [sic] the Government to give immediate consideration to previous plans and to expedite the construction of a landing area on the Island which will be available to the flying public." Though Howland's airstrip was not being built for AE alone, the preferential treatment was certainly a boost to her plans.

Campbell was then ordered to stay on the island after the field was completed and until Earhart had used it in March, when he was to return to Honolulu with all equipment and personnel. Though there had been negotiations with the Navy on refueling and some obsolete Army equipment had been borrowed to work on the airfield, it is clear neither the Army nor the Navy initiated work at Howland.

The more planning AE and GP did for the world flight, the clearer it became that Amelia would not be able to fly the Electra solo and navigate at the same time, at least from Honolulu to Australia. After that, she seemed confident she could handle it by herself. With some reluctance, Amelia decided she would have to find a navigator. During the final months of 1936 candidates for the position were invited to the Putnam home in Rye, New York.

One of the first people to make the trip was explorer/pilot Bradford Washburn, who had written three boys' books for G. P. Putnam's Sons and two *National Geographic* articles on high mountain exploration. Before he was twenty-five Washburn had made four trips to climb the Alps and six to Alaska, repeatedly using aircraft. In 1936 he led the National Geographic/Pan American Airways flights to photograph Mt. McKinley from the air in a Lockheed Electra.

Washburn had come to know George Putnam, his publisher, very well. During that winter he received a phone call from GP to come to Rye to spend the night with him and AE—she had "something very interesting to discuss" with him. Washburn recalled the memorable visit.

At supper, Amelia told me that she was putting together plans for a round-the-world flight in the summer and that she was interviewing a number of people as possible navigators. The facts (told her by GP) that I was thoroughly familiar with radio, had done a good deal of exploratory flying, and knew the basics of celestial navigation interested her—and she wanted to discuss her plans with me.

After supper we spread a mass of maps on the floor of the living room and Amelia and I sat on the floor while she described her plan to me in great detail. As things later turned out, I'm now fascinated by the fact that, at that time, she planned to start out across the Atlantic, thence to Egypt, India, Thailand, Java, northern Australia, Howland Island, Hawaii and San Francisco.

Her plan all seemed to make reasonable good sense to me except for her plan for navigation between Darwin, Australia, and Howland Island. All of her previous transoceanic flights (and all the earlier legs of this proposed flight) involved flying over or to points where there were operating radio stations on the ground. She had used a directional loop to home in on these points and therefore had run into no navigational problems that I knew of.

I asked her how she planned to hit Howland at the end of a 2000-mile flight *without a single intermediate emergency-landing spot*. She simply replied: Dead reckoning and star-and-sun sights. Howland Island, as I remember it, is a sliver of land in an immense mass of trackless ocean—about a mile and a half long and a half-mile wide. We never even got to discussing where she was going to land—on a beach or a small specially-prepared field. At that point *my problem wasn't landing*; it was *how to get there!*

I'd made a number of flights in the Lockheed Electra that she planned to use, as this was the aircraft with which we had made all of our Mt. McKinley flights in Alaska the previous summer. I pointed out that, as I recollected it, this airplane cruised most economically at about 9,000 feet, using two Pratt & Whitney Wasp engines. This would seem to give visibility over a reasonably wide sweep of ocean—*if it was cloudless*. But even in excellent weather, I pointed out, the Pacific rapidly develops an intricate pattern of fracto-cumulus clouds almost every morning, as soon as the sun rises high enough to heat the surface of the ocean. This would make it extremely difficult (if not impossible) to see a small island from 9–12,000 feet in the air.

It would either be obscured by the clouds, or badly confused with cloud-shadows which are usually very convincing "islands" until you approach them closely. This island was flat as a pancake with no mountains on it at all. Furthermore, if one went below the clouds as the flight neared its end, this would greatly reduce her horizon and vastly increase fuel consumption.

I insisted that some sort of radio transmitter was badly needed on that island, onto which she could lock her RDF loop as soon as she came into reasonable range. Amelia insisted that it wasn't necessary and when I stubbornly said that it was, GP, who was seated nearby looking down at us, said: "If we have to get radio equipment all the way out there, there wouldn't be any chance of getting your book out for the Christmas sale."

I replied that a big complex radio station wasn't at all necessary— just an automatic signal sent out continually—any sort of a signal that you could pick up with a Radio Direction Finder. If she had asked for a young radio-man to do this she'd have had hundreds of volunteers in a moment. In fact, she was so popular I'm sure that she'd have found a score of very competent operators who would have *paid her* for the fun and privilege of doing it. But Amelia simply insisted that it was just plain unnecessary and we went to bed on that note.

I returned to Boston by the morning train and I never heard from GP or Amelia again. The rumor has circulated for years that I was asked to be her navigator and refused. My response to this story is very simple: I was never asked. I was interviewed and found it very fascinating, but equally frustrating—particularly in view of what I suggested and what I knew she wanted to do.

Amelia and GP continued to search for a navigator, finally settling upon Harry Manning, the American President Lines ship captain who had explained the rudiments of celestial navigation to AE on the way back from England in 1928.

By the end of 1936 everything seemed well in order for the flight. Amelia and George accepted Floyd and Jackie Cochran Odlum's invitation to welcome New Year 1937 quietly at their Indio, California, ranch.

During this break from lectures and flight preparation, Jackie took the time to express what many of Amelia's friends felt: they were not in favor of the world flight because of its inherent risks. Amelia acknowledged that, on the whole, she could not deny their rational arguments to call it off, but she simply had to go ahead. It was a compulsion that had grown into an obsession, and nothing would deter her.

Amelia with her father, Edwin Stanton Earhart. His alcoholism eventually led to a divorce from Amy Otis Earhart, who never remarried.

June 1928—Amelia and Wilmer "Bill" Stultz in Halifax, Nova Scotia, after arriving with mechanic Louis "Slim" Gordon in the Fokker *Friendship*, which can be spotted in the distance. During the thirteen-day layover in Trepassey, Newfoundland, Stultz stayed drunk most of the time; Earhart had to get him up and walk him to the aircraft to make the flight. *National Archives*

The Fokker *Friendship,* in which Amelia became the first woman to cross the Atlantic by air, rests on the Solent at Southampton, England, June 19, 1928, the day after the flight. *National Archives*

Paul Mantz with Amelia and the Lockheed Vega just before the 1934 Bendix race. Mantz, an accomplished Hollywood stunt pilot, served as her technical adviser from 1934 until she was lost in 1937. He often had major differences of opinion with her husband, particularly over Amelia's having enough time to fly. *National Air and Space Museum*

Two of the most accomplished pilots of the 1930s, Wiley Post and Roscoe Turner, with Amelia in California. When Post warned her planned flight from Mexico to New York across the Gulf of Mexico was too dangerous, Amelia "could scarcely wait to be on my way." *National Air and Space Museum*

Amy Earhart and her daughter on January 15, 1935, just after the solo Pacific flight. *National Archives*

The red Vega being serviced at Wheeler Field, Hawaii, in January 1935. When she made the flight from Honolulu to Oakland, California, Amelia became the first person to solo anywhere in the Pacific and the first person to solo both the Atlantic and Pacific oceans. *Fred Corning*

With the purchase of Lockheed 10 Electra #1055, NR16020, through Purdue University, Amelia had the capability to make the flight she had dreamed of—around the world at the equator. Here she inspects her "flying laboratory" at the factory as it is being built, May 28, 1936. *National Archives*

George Putnam, Amelia's husband and manager, greets Amelia in Newark, New Jersey, on May 8, 1935, 2100 miles and 14 hours, 18 minutes and 30 seconds after leaving Mexico City.
National Archives

February 1937—at the press conference to announce the world flight. From left to right are Paul Mantz, Amelia, Harry Manning and Frederick Noonan. Originally Amelia intended to make the world flight solo, then reluctantly took on Manning and later Noonan as navigators for the initial Pacific legs. *National Air and Space Museum*

March 20, 1937—as the Electra gained speed down the runway at Luke Field, Hawaii, it began to drift to one side. Amelia countered by jockeying the throttles, something Mantz had told her never to do. The Electra ground-looped, doing a fair amount of damage. Here Mantz stands in the cockpit talking with Amelia and Fred on the left wing.

eft: One of the first candidates for navigator to accompany Earhart on her orld flight was Bradford Washburn, seen standing in front of a Lockheed 10 in airbanks, Alaska, in July 1936, when he led the National Geographic Society/ an American Airways photo flights over Mt. McKinley. Because of lack of roper radio equipment, Washburn did not want to take part in the flight. *ational Geographic Society via Washburn*

Greeting Fred and Amelia at Caripito were Standard's general manager, Henry E. Linam, and Pan American Airways manager Harry Drake (glasses). Harry and Fred had been roommates in Miami when they worked for Pan Am. Of their time together, Harry recalled later, "Many were the nights I carried him home and rolled him into bed dead drunk!" Noonan was later fired from the airline because of his alcoholism. *National Air and Space Museum*

Personnel pushed the Lockheed into the Standard/Pan Am hangar for the night.
National Air and Space Museum

Dinner in the Caripito hangar with company employees and their families. Note the Pratt & Whitney engine crate in the background. *National Air and Space Museum*

One June 21, 1937, the Electra arrived at Bandoeng, Java, after fighting its way through severe monsoon rains. One of the escorting Hawker Hind biplanes comes in to land as the Electra taxis in. *Claude E. Hartford—National Air and Space Museum*

Though radio navigation was by
far the most reliable way to reach
Howland, Amelia and Fred had little practical knowledge of its use.
Neither knew Morse code, so they
relied upon voice and did not know
the basics of using direction finders. *National Air and Space Museum*

The Coast Guard cutter *Itasca* was anchored
off Howland to help Amelia find the island. A
bearing on the Electra was never obtained.
National Archives

Left: Arrival at Lae, June 29, 1937, after 7
hours and 43 minutes in the air. The next leg
would be the most hazardous—to tiny
Howland Island.

The Japanese Imperial Navy service vessel *Koshu* sailed for the Marshall Islands on July 9, 1937. The night of July 13 she took on coal at Jaluit, then steamed for Mili Atoll, where Earhart, Noonan and the Electra were picked up.

Captain Vincent V. Loomis, USAF (center), and some of the men under his command in the Pacific, 1952.

Queen Bosket Diklan of Mili Atoll. Married to the Japanese commander of the atoll, Takinami, in 1937, she remembered the Electra coming down and its crew being captured.

Japanese medical corpsman Bilimon Amaran was called to the ship in Jaluit harbor along with the health services commander in 1937 to treat a white man with blue eyes. The American had sustained head and knee injuries in the crash of his aircraft, piloted by a white woman. Their silver twin-engine aircraft was seen by Amaran on the fantail of the ship, missing one wing.

Vince Loomis on Mili, 1979.

Paul Rafford, Jr., in 1940 as a twenty-one-year-old radio operator with Pan American Airways. His experience with the radio equipment and practices of the 1930s helped him discover why the Electra did not find Howland Island. *Pan American Airlines via Paul Rafford, Jr.*

This is the spot near Barre Island, Mili Atoll, where the Electra ditched on a reef about 100 yards offshore. Several Marshallese saw the aircraft come down.

Failing to dissuade her, Jackie urged Amelia at least to give Manning a practical test of his abilities. AE could not ignore Jackie's request; both women had experimented with extrasensory perception, and at least twice Jackie revealed that she had knowledge of things in Amelia's life she could have known in no other way.

As soon as Amelia got back to Burbank, she took Manning far out over the Pacific in the Electra and asked him to chart a course back to Los Angeles. What actually happened depends upon which of the two stories is accurate. Amelia said the captain miscalculated by 200 miles. Manning said it was Amelia who was off course, and that she tended to drift to the left consistently when trying to follow a heading. Regardless, both sides agreed an assistant navigator would be a wise precaution, at least for the initial east-to-west Pacific legs. The best choice seemed to be Frederick J. Noonan, one of the finest navigators employed, until recently, at Pan Am.

Noonan had begun his career as a seventeen-year-old seaman. After World War I he started flying as a navigator with Pan Am and soon won a reputation as a natural at the intricacies of celestial navigation. Not only had he been the inspector of all Pan Am bases and the navigator of the famous China Clipper beginning November 1935, but he had been given the job of mapping the new Far East–Pacific routes for the company.

By early 1937, however, Fred Noonan was out of a job and looking for work, and no one in the aviation industry would touch him. Though he could navigate better than most, he had been fired by Pan Am because of his addiction to alcohol. Harry Drake, who had shared a bachelor apartment with Fred, later recalled their friendship. Both got along well, but Harry summed up Fred's problem to fellow Pan Am employee Paul Rafford: "Many were the nights I carried him home and rolled him into bed dead drunk!"

Pilots who flew with Noonan on the San Francisco-to-Hawaii route told Rafford that Fred's procedure was to set up his charts at the beginning of the flight and then retire to the lavatory with his briefcase. Later, after doing some work at the navigation table for an hour or so, he would again disappear. Finally, after this routine had been repeated several times, he would have to be guided to a bunk to sleep off his stupor while the rest of the crew filled in for him.

Amelia was warned about him, but since he was only assisting Manning, there was not a great deal to worry about. When Fred Noonan was sober, he was among the finest airmen in the world, and he promised Amelia he would stay sober. Besides, the plan was just for Noonan to assist on the leg to Howland and then get off, while Manning navigated the route to Sydney. From there AE would fly the rest of the way solo. The warnings about Noonan were to Amelia like so many others she would encounter: useless baggage.

Louise Thaden had grave misgivings about the world flight. The two pilots had been friends since 1929, and Louise knew the flight "had been a secret ambition for years. As far as I know it is the only major flight she ever attempted for purely selfish reasons. She wanted to fly around the world, because it would be fun." In January 1937 Louise flew to Burbank to look over the Lockheed and have some time alone to talk AE out of making the flight. Amelia's response was firm: "I've wanted to do this flight for a long time. I've worked hard and I deserve *one* fling during my life time."

Thaden, in recalling that meeting, found it "impossible adequately to describe her staunch fineness, her clear-eyed honesty, her unbiased fairness, the undefeated spirit, the calm resourcefulness, her splendid mentality, the nervous reserve which has carried her through exhausting flights and more exhausting lecture tours." Yet this time many were worried that nervous reserve would not carry her through this last try at an aviation record. Amelia made it clear that after this flight she was going to give up "stunt" flying.

On January 31, 1937, Manning was named as navigator for the world flight with Noonan as assistant. Commander Clarence Williams had prepared the maps and routes, while Jacques de Sibour of Standard Oil of New Jersey, assisted by Bob Oertel, worked out how a supply of fuel and oil could be "spotted" for her around the world. Official announcement of the flight came on February 12.

Apparently Paul Mantz's and Brad Washburn's insistence on the need for radio navigation had gotten through to someone.

W. L. Smith, Pacific Coast representative for Western Electric, wrote Mantz's United Air Services on January 28 that the necessary equipment for radio direction-finding on 500 kilocycles (an emergency marine frequency not normally used in aviation) could be provided. The Electra 13A 50-watt radio transmitter and 20B receiver would have to be modified by Bell Telephone Laboratories, but that would take only four weeks. F. C. McMullen of Bell, who had sent Smith the details on the conversion, emphasized in his wire of the same day that "in order to obtain satisfactory results on 500 kilocycles a trailing wire at least 250 feet long should be used."

As expenses mounted, GP headed back across country to raise more funds. A few airlines contributed, but the major boost came from Gimbels in New York when the store agreed to sell letter covers that Amelia would carry with her and mail back to collectors after she landed at the various stops. Much to GP's delight, 10,000 of them were purchased, adding more than $25,000 to the bank account.

With takeoff planned for March 15 from Oakland, Mantz gave up his motion-picture work in February to devote all his time to the effort. The Electra was in excellent shape, but Paul continued to worry about Amelia's lack of experience with the ship. He suggested that a cross-country trip from Los Angeles to New York and back to Oakland would be ideal for sharpening her twin-engine technique, but AE thought it a waste of time. Besides, she did not want to put extra hours on the engines. Her alternative was to have Paul along for the first leg, from Oakland to Honolulu. Mantz accepted this idea as the best he could do.

By early March the Electra and the crew were in place in Oakland, but on the thirteenth heavy rains made it obvious the proposed departure date would most likely slide by. Finally, at 4:00 P.M. on March 17, conditions had cleared enough to allow the Electra to be pulled out of the Navy hangar. Paul climbed aboard and began a series of engine checks, then taxied to the end of the 7000-foot runway after Manning and Noonan settled in at the chart table. As with the other flights that had been made from Oakland, there was no announcement as to whether this was "it" or just another practice flight.

Amelia was driven to the end of the runway in a Navy staff car.

Waving goodbye to George, she climbed up into the right seat. On takeoff Paul handled the throttles and landing gear while Amelia took the flight controls. As he eased the throttles full forward, Mantz yelled over, "Never jockey the throttles. Hold her straight with the rudder and push everything to the firewall, smoothly!" The Electra lifted off at 4:37 P.M. with plenty of room to spare.

At 8000 feet Amelia leveled off and Paul set cruise power on the engines; then they switched seats so she could fly the ocean as pilot in command with her adviser looking on. For fifty minutes of every hour, Earhart flew while Mantz kept a log of radio contacts, fuel consumption and cloud cover; then Mantz would spell her for ten minutes. An hour out, they passed the Pan Am Clipper flown by Ed Musick. That was a noteworthy experience for Amelia, since rarely did aircraft cross paths in the sky—and it was the first time she had seen another aircraft at sea. She found out later that none of Pan Am's pilots had ever seen another plane en route over the ocean either.

Three hours out, AE and Paul shared some cocoa, a welcome relief; she had been doing most of the flying through some rough rain squalls. Mantz was pleased with her performance. Poor weather came just as night fell, but AE stayed on the controls without letting the Electra get away from her. If she could hold course within a few degrees as she was doing, then she'd have no problem with the rest of the trip. Manning and Noonan stayed very busy in the green-blue light of the aft cabin, plotting and re-plotting the course to the islands.

Numerous times Manning had to make his way forward over the fuel tanks to use the radio and shoot star sights through the upper hatch. Each time Amelia had to let Paul fly as she leaned down and Harry worked over her head. Mantz realized the navigation hatch should have been fitted over the chart room, but hindsight didn't help.

The Sperry autopilot proved to be a fine aid as the horizon became indistinct. This was the first time AE had flown with one, calling it her "little helper." The radios worked very well, with extensive range, and the crew of the Electra was in contact with someone almost all the time.

Toward the end of the flight Paul noticed that Amelia was tiring rapidly, even with the aid of the autopilot and himself. Without a copilot to take some of the strain, how would she do? He could only bury the thought by noting how well things were going.

As they came within range of the Makapuu radio beacon on Oahu, Noonan asked AE to keep it 10 degrees to the right of the airplane's nose. This was another first for her: prior to this flight she had never used the recently developed radio direction finder. (Washburn had been mistaken.) AE rotated the antenna loop atop the cockpit until she got a null in the earphones. She turned the Electra onto the bearing indicated by the needle and then turned left 10 degrees. This would be the wind drift correction for the course Noonan had figured to fly them to Hawaii.

When the Makapuu radio operators asked for a transmission from the Electra in order to locate the aircraft, Manning held the telegraph key down so the carrier wave could be picked up and tracked. Normally a transmission of more than a minute was required to complete the process, but the generator could not deliver the required power long enough and burned out. At least the other generator powering the DF worked, so it was not vital that they home in on Makapuu—but what would happen if AE needed a steer during the trip and the generator did the same thing?

Mantz had run through his calculated cruise power settings very carefully, using the Cambridge fuel analyzer to compute the exact fuel consumption. After using 60 gallons per hour (gph) the first three hours, he gradually reduced consumption down to 38 gph at a true air speed of 150 mph. Amelia would have to adhere to Paul's cruise tables religiously if she was going to make those long legs, but even with an unusually high average fuel consumption of 50 gph, the Electra had a time aloft of more than twenty-four hours carrying its total capacity of 1202 gallons.

Eighty miles out, Noonan gave the word Amelia could start a let-down. Drained from the flight and feeling its effects, she turned to Paul and asked him to take the ship in for a landing. Mantz later recalled to Don Dwiggins, "I went around Makapuu point and then crossed Wheeler Field. I wrapped it around in a steep bank to check the wind sock. AE yelled, 'Don't! Don't!' She was very fatigued and kind of exuberant. She calmed down when I made a normal approach pattern and we landed."

Because she suffered recurring bouts of illness after long periods of stress, Amelia clearly was not an ideal candidate for long-distance flying. The tension of long flights could easily lead to such exhaustion that her judgment would become impaired. This did not bode well for the forthcoming flight, certainly the most difficult of her career.

The Electra touched down at Wheeler Field 15 hours and 52 minutes, and 2410 miles, after leaving Oakland, with more than four hours' worth of fuel aboard of the 947 gallons carried, much to Mantz's credit. In spite of her fatigue, Amelia hoped to press on for Howland, but the weather did not cooperate. As in 1935, Chris and Mona Holmes put Amelia up; after sleeping for six hours she sunbathed the rest of her exhaustion away. Mantz found his fiancée, Terry Minor, waiting for him. Amelia was delighted, feeling a bit like Cupid, having delivered the lovers to each other.

Early the next morning Mantz flew the Electra from Wheeler to Luke Field, where the longer runway would give a greater margin of safety for takeoff when the plane was fully loaded. Wilbur Thomas, Pratt & Whitney's Hawaiian representative, fussed over the engines to make sure they were in top condition, and Mantz purchased 590 gallons of high-octane military fuel, giving the Electra a total of 900 gallons for the 1800-mile hop to Howland.

The Coast Guard cutter *Itasca* was stationed off Howland after having carried Earhart's supplies and two Navy mechanics to the island. The ship would act as a "plane guard" to help guide Amelia in if necessary.

On the morning of March 20 AE was aboard the Electra with Noonan at the chart table and Manning in the copilot's seat. Mantz waited anxiously on the ramp at Luke along with mostly military personnel, including Brigadier General Barton K. Yount, who had gathered to watch the start of the 1800-mile leg to Howland. Engine run-up was completed, and AE signaled for the chocks to be pulled from the wheels at 7:35 A.M. Taxiing out to the wet runway, she centered the Lockheed and slowly advanced the throttles. There was a slight crosswind.

As the aircraft gained speed, Mantz could see it start to drift to one side and involuntarily cried out to his student, "Don't jockey those throttles!" Amelia later recalled,

> Suddenly the plane pulled to my right. I reduced the power on the opposite engine and succeeded in swinging from the right to the left. For a moment I thought I would be able to gain control and straighten the course. But, alas, the load was so heavy, once it started an arc there was nothing to do but let the plane ground loop as easily as possible.
>
> With the excessive weight, the landing gear on the right was wrenched free and gasoline sprayed from the drain-well. That there was no fire was surely the result of the generous good wishes which had come to me from all over the world.

AE switched off the ignition immediately, avoiding further possibility of fire, and Paul jumped on the first available vehicle as ambulances and fire trucks raced to the wreck. Amelia was following Fred and Harry out just as Paul arrived. "I don't know what happened, Paul," she said, her face drained of color.

As Don Dwiggins later recorded, "Mantz put his arm around her shoulders. 'That's all right, Amelia. So long as nobody was hurt. You just didn't listen to Papa, did you?' Amelia smiled wanly and shook her head. She'd learned the hard way not to jockey the throttles." Though Amelia later found it very difficult to admit she had mismanaged the throttles, her account clearly shows she tried to halt the swerve the wrong way. The only course of action, as Mantz had told her many times, was to jerk the throttles back to idle and then settle the aircraft down.

Though both propellers and landing gear were washed out and the right wing and vertical stabilizer bent, the Electra was in much better shape than it had first appeared. Amelia, with George's support, decided quickly the world flight attempt would be resumed as soon as the aircraft was repaired. Mantz arranged to have the machine disassembled and shipped back to Lockheed in Burbank. AE, Fred and Harry were aboard the cruise ship *Malolo* by noon on the day of the crash, bound for California.

Manning made it quite clear that he did not wish to make the trip when it was tried again. News releases said Manning's leave from his company was up; that was not the case. He later recalled the aftermath of the accident. "Amelia was responsible for the crash [in Hawaii] . . . overcorrected to the left, then to the right, gas leaking, sparks. We were all just damn lucky it didn't catch fire. AE was something of a prima donna—had an ego and could be as tough as nails. I got very fed up with her bullheadedness several times. That's why she brought Noonan into the picture— in the event that I gave up on the flight. . . . AE was not a good navigator. Fred Noonan was a happy-go-lucky Irishman. He was not a constant navigator. I always felt he let things go far too long."

On the ship back to California Amelia was faced with the loss of Manning and the realization that problems could crop up without warning. Apparently she decided aboard ship that she would not make the flight solo but with Noonan if he could be relied upon. When she asked Fred if he wanted to go along as the sole navigator, he replied, "I do. I need this flight."

"All the way?" she inquired.

"Do you trust me?" he shot back.

"I believe in you," she replied.

This former social worker's faith in an alcoholic's ability to overcome his disease had been strongly reflected in her faith in her father and in Bill Stultz, who had come out of a stupor to get the *Friendship* across the Atlantic in 1928. Amelia asked about Fred's forthcoming wedding, and he admitted that the major problem would be staying away from his habit. "Does she know about your battle with the bottle?" AE asked.

"Yes," Noonan replied, "but I think I can win with her."

Fred Noonan and his fiancée were married on March 27, the same day the Electra left Hawaii. But apparently the habit still plagued him. Shortly after the wedding, Fred and his bride crashed into another car near Fresno, California. The police cited him for driving in the wrong lane and noted on his traffic ticket: "No injuries. Driver had been drinking."

Lockheed estimated it would take $25,000 and at least five weeks to repair the Electra, pushing the start of the flight into mid-May.

This meant that AE would be coming home across the Atlantic, at the earliest, in late June, possibly early July. Average weather conditions in the Caribbean and Africa during that period were considered unfavorable, so the direction of the flight was reversed. It would be made from west to east, from Oakland to Miami, then South America, across Africa, India and Southeast Asia, then down to Australia and New Guinea, to Howland and Honolulu, ending up in Oakland. For some reason, this route reversal was not made public until just before the second attempt.

Another $25,000 had to be raised for respotting fuel and provisions along the reversed route, and GP needed to beat the bushes again. On April 25 Amelia was back at Gimbels in New York with her revised set of 10,000 "2nd Take Off" letter covers, announcing the flight would be launched again in mid-May with Fred Noonan as sole navigator. When asked how much the flight was costing her, she made no attempt to hide the fact it was stretching all of her resources. "Well, I'm mortgaging the future—but then, what are futures for?" Many of her friends, including Bernard Baruch, Richard Byrd and the Odlums, pitched in with personal donations, some quite large.

While Amelia seemed happy with the way things were going, Paul Mantz and George Putnam were butting heads harder than ever. Paul thought AE listened to her husband too much, while GP said she didn't listen to him enough.

In addition, Amelia was determined to back Fred Noonan's desire to run a navigator's school after the flight by giving him permission to use her name, something GP never did unless there was a direct royalty involved. George had never been in favor of keeping Noonan aboard through the entire flight, since he thought it would rob AE of some of the glory. He wanted her to go solo the last few (and certainly the most dangerous) legs. Amelia made it clear Noonan would be aboard for the entire trip.

The most important use of radio would be during the leg inbound to Howland Island. The cutter *Itasca* was reassigned off the island for the second attempt; its job was to locate the Electra with its radio direction finders and then give AE the correct compass heading. The Bendix loop antenna mounted in the aircraft by Mantz would enable Amelia to home in on the *Itasca*'s transmissions. This loop would receive the strongest signal when its axis was at right angles to the direction of the station. By rotating it slowly, AE could listen and hear when signal strength dropped to minimum, or null; at that point the loop axis would be pointing at the station. Since the 6210- and 3105-kilocycle frequencies were very ineffective for this type of DF work, the medium-wave 500-kilocycle frequency, then in use for emergency SOS calls from ships at sea, would make it much easier. Mantz had covered the bases well.

Although her radios were the best that could be obtained in 1937, Amelia was ambivalent toward them. Moreover, Noonan distrusted the creeping tide of new gadgets that were making an ever-increasing impact upon aviation. A seat-of-the-pants navigator, albeit a very good one, he believed he would not need to rely on the radios and their direction-finding abilities to stay on course.

Fred had developed his attitude through some bad experiences. As his friend and fellow crewmate Captain Marius Lodeesen recalled, while inbound to Oakland their Pan Am Clipper had brushed the trees of Mt. Tamalpais, shrouded in fog. This near-tragic mistake was traced to a faulty direction finder at Oakland that gave them a bearing 40 degrees in error. After Lodeesen landed the Clipper on the bay, Fred remarked, "Lodi, if we had gone in, my name would have gone down as the world's lousiest navigator." Lodeesen mused nearly fifty years later, "Fate, in the end, did just that."

Apparently Amelia's attitude matched Fred's, reflected in her meeting with the Pan American officials just before the flight got under way. Pan Am agreed to give Amelia all the help it could, both operational and technical. One of the company's engineers described those efforts to radio operator Paul Rafford. At one of the planning meetings that engineer had suggested that she carry the tuning crystal for a Pan Am frequency in her transmitter. This could give their ground direction-finding stations a chance to follow her across the Pacific and fix her position at regular intervals for possible rescue efforts. "This was a standard practice with Pan Am flights in those days," said Rafford, "and we routinely transmitted a two-minute dash twice an hour for the DF stations. The radio fixes so obtained were a useful aid in backing up our navigator's positions obtained by dead reckoning and celestial sights."

The only way the Pan Am frequency could be incorporated was to drop one of the existing crystals from the Electra's radio, but the plan never got that far. Before any further explanation, Amelia snapped, "I don't need that. I've got a navigator to tell me where I am!" The engineer was taken aback; he had not expected such a reaction. The subject was closed and the meeting ended.

On May 17 Lockheed put the finishing touches on the Electra, and the next day Amelia flew it to look for "bugs." With GP and mechanic Bo McKneely aboard, AE brought the aircraft to Oakland, where Noonan was waiting, on May 19. The press made a number of guesses as to when the actual flight would start, but Amelia would only say there were other test flights to make before the actual departure. In fact, this was the truth as Mantz saw it. He wanted to check the radio equipment one last time and run a series of fuel-consumption flights in order to give Amelia the optimum power settings for each leg.

On May 21 Amelia, GP, Noonan and McKneely climbed aboard the Lockheed and took off for another "shakedown flight." This time the aircraft did not return; it was bound for Miami without a word to anyone that the around-the-world flight had actually started.

Paul learned of the departure from a commercial radio broadcast while he was in St. Louis with Tex Rankin at an aerobatic competition. As his biographer, Dwiggins, recorded, Mantz "was furious. AE was not ready! He smelled disaster. 'You're worrying too hard, Paul,' Rankin said reassuringly. 'She'll make it.' Mantz was far from convinced. She'd been pushing too hard, trying to meet the tight schedules set up by her promoter-husband. Too much attention had been given to the money-making schemes—advertising gimmicks . . . books . . . screenplays . . . public appearances . . . endorsements. Amelia had little time to devote to her flight preparation. She'd left it all up to Paul."

Now Amelia would be flying by guesswork instead of the careful procedures Paul had wanted to write down for her to follow. A nagging fear started to haunt Mantz from that moment—that he had not done enough to prepare Earhart for the flight.

Outbound from Oakland, Amelia surely felt none of the concern of her mentor in St. Louis. She was supremely confident that all would go just as expected. She landed at Tucson after what she recalled as a "leisurely afternoon flight."

After landing and checking in, Amelia started the engines to taxi to the fuel pit. The left Pratt & Whitney engine backfired and burst into flames. Though the fire threatened to spread out of control, AE pulled the handle connected to the Lux extinguisher mounted in the engine section and the blaze puffed out. Word soon spread that Earhart had made a dramatic arrival, and reporters came away saying that the aircraft would be flown back to Los Angeles for repairs.

When McKneely examined the accessory section, he found the fire to have been relatively minor. On May 22 they flew on to New Orleans, where George left the flight and took a train to New York. The next day the Electra and its crew went on to Miami. Meeting reporters again, Amelia said she was undecided about where to go next, since she was only testing the aircraft, but most likely the "party will return to California after repairs are completed."

For over a week McKneely and others, including Pan Am mechanics, worked on the aircraft to get it ready for the initial leg of the world flight, to San Juan, Puerto Rico. Though press reports and photos showed Amelia happily in the midst of the mechanics, one of them remembered closing the cowling on one of the engines and not having enough time to wipe off his greasy handprints when Earhart came out to the flight line to see how things were going. When she saw the mess "she swore at me with curse words I didn't believe any woman even knew!"

The repairs AE discussed with reporters were primarily involved with the radios, which proved to be a source of continual trouble. This would not have been a surprise to Mantz, who had wanted to work on them until they were right. Before leaving St. Louis for California, Paul sent an air-mail letter to Putnam in New York, asking if everything was in order. GP's reply of June 3 was waiting for him when he arrived in Burbank: "Talked with Amelia on the telephone at San Juan from Miami. She says that at last they got the Sperry [autopilot] really working perfectly. Between ourselves, the radio gave unending trouble. As I understand it, it was finally decided by the technicians that the longer aerials were improper. One part of them just cancelled out the other, so they shortened the aerials and apparently got the thing pretty well licked."

Somehow GP's reply wasn't very comforting to Mantz; the reply rambled on about how great Putnam thought it was that Mantz had done well in the recent aerobatic meet, but the tone of the letter was casual, even evasive. Mantz decided to probe the boys at Pan Am in Miami a bit more.

When he did, he found that, among other things, Earhart and Noonan had decided to leave the telegraph key and the trailing antenna behind. They explained that since neither was proficient in Morse code, it would just be excess baggage.

Mantz was stunned. He knew AE had always hated reeling the 250-foot trailing antenna in and out, but now it had been removed, along with the telegraph key, ostensibly to save a few pounds in weight. Mantz's effort to assure Amelia the opportunity to be tracked in an emergency was now of no account. She would be on her own. How many more chances could she take?

DF steers would have to be done by Earhart herself with her own radio on very inefficient frequencies. An experimental Army DF had been sent with the *Itasca* to Howland by Lieutenant Daniel A. Cooper at Mantz's urging, but it would have to be operated on the island with borrowed batteries. At least the ship itself had an excellent radio set-up, but Amelia's contempt for the use of radio gave no reason for optimism. Would she know what to do with hers even if everything was set up properly?

In thinking back over Earhart's failure to appreciate the use of radio, Brad Washburn was amazed that "for some reason unknown to all of us, she refused to use a 'trailing' antenna, a disastrous mistake in her technical planning. This greatly reduced the range of her reception. For some weird reason she hated trailing antennas. The small 'doublet' [antenna] that she used (from the tip of each wing to the tail) forced her into transmitting with rather high [inefficient] frequencies." He went on to explain that "by having that terribly short antenna system, she vastly reduced the number of people who might conceivably pick her up."

On June 1, 1937, at 5:56 A.M., Amelia Earhart and Fred

Noonan lifted off from Miami Municipal Airport for San Juan. Amelia had told her friend Carl Allen of the New York *Herald Tribune*, "I have a feeling there is just about one more good flight left in my system, and I hope this trip is it. Anyway, when I have finished this job, I mean to give up long-distance 'stunt' flying."

Chapter 4

Last Flight

1937

GEORGE PUTNAM, along with his son David, Bo McKneely and the Miami Airport personnel, watched the Electra disappear into a cloudless early-morning sky. Confidence ran high among those who had helped Amelia and Fred prepare for the first leg to Puerto Rico. Only a few of the Pan Am technicians brooded over Earhart's lack of interest in what their airline's radio network could do to ensure the flight's success. Regardless, they had fine-tuned the radio equipment as well as they could and hoped for the best. By the time Mantz received Putnam's letter of June 3, telling of the radio problems and leaving the trailing antenna behind, he was simply another spectator to AE's world attempt.

While Amelia flew the Electra past the Bahamas, enjoying the scenery, Noonan took no time to sightsee as he busily plotted points below to check their course and ground speed. Amelia enjoyed hearing about her takeoff on Miami's WQAM, the radio station selected to deliver Pan Am's hourly weather summary.

By midmorning Fred estimated arrival at San Juan at 1:10 P.M. Amelia was filled with confidence now that the flight was finally under way. She recorded her impressions of the round-the-world trip in *Last Flight.*

I remembered a few days earlier, while we were still far from land flying across the Gulf of Mexico he had predicted we would sight Tampa at 12:10. Actually we made our landfall one minute earlier. So I had come to have implicit faith in my shipmate's powers of divination.

What with such expert navigational help and the assistance of the Sperry gyro-pilot, I began to feel that my long-range flying was becoming pretty sissy. The ease and casualness were further accentuated by the marvelous help given by radio. Were I alone on such a trip as this, I would be hopping along shorelines, my attention divided between flying the ship and attempting to keep track of exactly where I was.

Seven hours and thirty-three minutes after leaving Florida, the Electra touched down in Puerto Rico. In spite of Amelia's praise for her navigator, he was nineteen minutes off in his estimated time of arrival. No explanation was given in her log for the discrepancy, which was the first of several navigational problems that would plague the flight.

While Pan Am took care of the plane and fiddled with the radios a bit more, Amelia and Fred were taken under fellow pilot Clara Livingston's wing to avoid the eyes of the curious and get some rest. Before getting to bed at 8:00 P.M., AE called her husband to fill him in on how things were going.

The next morning AE was out of bed at 3:45 and took off shortly before 7:00 for Caripito, Venezuela; the airfield there was managed jointly by Pan Am and Standard Oil. After landing at Caripito and receiving a warm greeting from Venezuelan officials, the flyers attended a lunch hosted in the hangar by Henry E. Linam, Standard's general manager for the area.

The manager of the Pan Am station there was none other than Fred's old roommate Harry Drake. He had been instructed by the company to give the world travelers all the help he could, so that night Harry told Amelia he would meet her and Fred just before takeoff with the latest en route weather and airport information.

Earhart brushed him off with a curt, "But I don't need any of that stuff. I got it all back in California before I left."

Harry gulped and then replied, "But ma'am, your information must be weeks old and out of date." Drake had set up a special series of radio schedules with Pan Am stations on the east coast of South America, and he wasn't about to let everything go unused. He sat up all night gathering the information he had promised.

With dawn rapidly approaching, Harry jumped into his car and drove to the airport. Just as he pulled onto the access road, he heard the roar of engines and then watched in disgust as the

Electra disappeared in the distance. As he shook his head in disbelief, the thought struck him, "I wonder if I'll ever see Fred alive again?"

Pressing through rain clouds, Amelia climbed to 8000 feet and topped most of the weather. Strong headwinds cut ground speed down to an average of 148 mph, which included dodging squalls and then letting back down over the dense jungle to fly under the monstrous black clouds as the storms grew to gigantic proportions and reached altitudes that were far above her airplane's capabilities. This time she was lucky; she somehow managed to fly on into clearing weather and land safely at Paramaribo, Dutch Guiana.

After getting the Lockheed attended to, Amelia and Fred boarded the railroad for town, where they were put up at one of Fred's old Pan Am hangouts, the Palace Hotel. Another of his friends, radio operator Carl Doake, was there. Amelia later said the South American legs were the most joyful for Fred, because he could see his former working companions.

From there the 1330 miles to Fortaleza, Brazil, were flown on June 4 over either open sea or dense jungle with few checkpoints. For the first time Amelia crossed the equator, something Fred had done on numerous occasions as a Master Mariner (the highest rating a navigator can receive). He was too involved with navigating to perform his duties as King Neptune and forgot to douse AE with a thermos bottle of cold water, part of the traditional first-equatorial-crossing ceremonies.

At Fortaleza, Amelia again found the Pan Am facility at her disposal, so she decided to stop for a day and make preparations for the South Atlantic hop there rather than at the actual takeoff point at Natal. A small fuel gauge leak was fixed, the oil was changed, everything was greased, and in general the aircraft was cleaned up. The crew also had a chance to get their clothes laundered. Amelia's total wardrobe consisted of "five shirts, two pairs of slacks, a change of shoes, a light working coverall and a trick weightless raincoat, plus the minimum of toilet articles." She thought this elaborate compared to flying the Atlantic with no luggage at all and no personal equipment but a toothbrush.

The short 270-mile flight to Natal was made early in the morning on June 6 with hopes of leaving for Africa the same day. Upon arrival AE asked the Air France pilots who made regular transoceanic crossings about the weather, which was regularly reported from two ships stationed in the South Atlantic. They suggested she wait until the next day, which meant anytime after midnight. This time she listened to their advice. But her impatience, as usual, lay just beneath the surface.

Those who helped get the airplane ready in Brazil had found Noonan's need for a few drinks quite normal. But several Pan Am employees later remembered that Noonan had seemed to retreat to the bottle for relief from what he felt was unjustifiable pushing from Amelia. In his eyes she had become a stern taskmaster. Though Fred had promised Amelia he would abstain from alcohol, he found the promise all but impossible to keep. It was obvious to those who hosted the two fliers that there was a growing tension between them, in spite of their external cordiality.

Not long after midnight, at 3:15 on the morning of June 7, AE pushed the throttles all the way forward, growling off into the night toward Dakar, Senegal. In spite of heavy rain and headwinds, AE's speed of 147 mph was only slightly short of the predicted speed, with power settings of 26.5 inches manifold pressure and 1700 rpm. For the entire world trip Mantz had given her a base speed of 150 mph for flight-planning purposes. This meant the engines would not have to be pushed. If necessary, power could be increased to gain 20 mph or more, but this would eat up more fuel.

About halfway across the Atlantic, the Electra passed the Air France mail plane. "Unfortunately I could not 'talk' to it. The mail plane's radio equipment, I believe, is telegraphic code, while mine, at the moment, was exclusively voice telephone. As always, I broadcast my position by voice each half hour. Whether it was heard at all, or understood if heard, perhaps I shall never know." In about three weeks this idle question would turn into a desperate plea over the Pacific.

During much of the crossing Fred "dozed," according to Amelia. (Those who knew Fred wondered if he wasn't hung over.) As a result, Amelia did much of her own navigating. By the time they approached the African coast, Noonan was on the job again. He indicated that Amelia should turn south toward Dakar. Either out of lack of trust in Noonan or out of stubbornness, she decided that it would be better to turn north. Amelia reckoned that the haze, which had made a position sighting difficult, called for her to trust her own instincts. She was wrong.

Finally, with night falling after 13 hours and 12 minutes of flying, she decided to land at a small jungle airstrip 163 miles off course, north of Dakar.

Deciding to delay the trip down to Dakar to avoid flying at night, AE got her first glimpse of African life. Her account of this experience reveals that she was a champion not only of women's equality but of equality between the races as well. "Tall black figures endowed with a certain innate dignity went about their own affairs without much concern for their neighbor airplanes. Seeing the majesty of these natives I asked myself what many must have asked before. What have we in the United States done to these proud people, so handsome and intelligent in the setting of their own country?"

The next morning, June 8, the Electra was flown south to Dakar, where the forty-hour check was run on the engines and a fuel meter, broken since two hours after they had left Natal, was fixed. Then, because of the probability of tornadoes, AE and Fred took the Lockheed to Gao in the French Sudan on the River Niger instead of to Niamey. Another overnight stay, with the typical before-dawn start, and they were off to Fort Lamy. Hops of 1000 miles were now routine, and the aircraft was doing exceptionally well.

Crossing Africa, however, was not an easy task, as Noonan wrote to his wife, Mary.

From a navigational aspect, our flights over the desert were more difficult than over water. That was because the maps of the country are very inaccurate and consequently extremely misleading. In fact, at points no dependence at all could be placed upon them. Also, recognizable landmarks are few and far between, one part of the desert being as much like another as two peas in a pod. However, we were lucky in always reaching our objectives. In all the distance I don't think we wandered off the course for half an hour, although there were times when I wouldn't have bet a nickle on the accuracy of our assumed position.

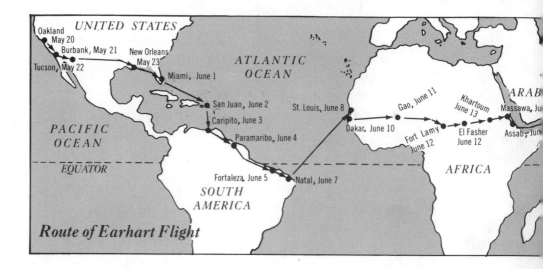

Route of Earhart Flight

Oakland
May 20
Burbank, May 21
Tucson, May 22
New Orleans
May 23
Miami, June 1
UNITED STATES
ATLANTIC
OCEAN
San Juan, June 2
Caripito, June 3
St. Louis, June 8
Paramaribo, June 4
PACIFIC
OCEAN
Gao, June 11
Khartoum
June 13
Massawa, Ju
ARAB
Dakar, June 10
Fort Lamy
June 12
El Fasher
June 12
Assab, Jun
EQUATOR
AFRICA
Fortaleza, June 5
Natal, June 7
SOUTH
AMERICA

By the evening of June 12 the flyers were at El Fasher, Anglo-Egyptian Sudan, after a bumpy ride in the oppressive heat. Here, as in most stops, officials waived as much red tape as possible and even conducted the disinfecting with "Flit guns" as gently as they could. (At each stop plane and crew had to be fumigated to prevent disease-carrying insects from hitchhiking.)

Through Sunday morning, June 13, the Lockheed flew deep into the Anglo-Egyptian Sudan and across an uncharted area on the map the size of an outstretched hand that had not one reference on it. The landing at Khartoum, on the Nile, in 110-degree heat was marked by great clouds of dust. With the help of cordial British officials, the Electra was serviced and no time was wasted in getting airborne for Massawa in Italy's Eritrea on the eastern edge of Africa. The temperature upon landing there was only 10 degrees lower, yet that did not stop airport personnel from swarming over the Electra. They could not speak English, but they had been briefed ahead of time on what they had to do.

On June 14 the Lockheed headed down the Red Sea for Assab to prepare for the long flight along the Arabian coast to India. Takeoff the next day was made well before daylight for staging through Aden; then the team headed for Karachi, where they arrived at 7:05 P.M. The 1920 miles from Assab had been flown in 13 hours and 10 minutes, slower than usual since the fuel-mixture

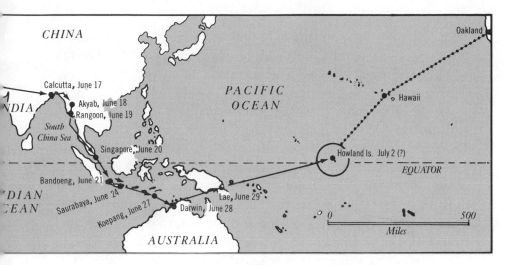

lever for the right engine had jammed, feeding too much fuel to the engine and forcing Amelia to slow down to conserve fuel.

In Karachi to meet her was Jacques de Sibour, who had been instrumental in getting maps, fuel, supplies and data in general to make the trip possible. He happily told her that a nonstop flight had never been made from the Red Sea to India. AE was delighted. "For me, who had never flown outside of North America (excepting a couple of oceans) this bit of far-away air adventuring was a deeply interesting experience."

After greetings had been taken care of, de Sibour told Amelia there was a phone call for her. Expecting a local reporter, she found GP on the wire 8274 miles away, on the other side of the world. She learned there had been a great deal of concern about her safety: her departure from Massawa had been announced over the news wires as a takeoff for Karachi, not Assab, and she had been reported 20 hours overdue there.

The two-day stay at Karachi allowed a good going-over for the plane and some much-needed rest for the crew. Pratt & Whitney had sent a crate of engine parts, allowing replacement of many important items for the first time on the trip.

—From Karachi on June 17 Amelia and Fred flew the Electra 1390 miles in 8½ hours to Calcutta, landing at Dum Dum field just before 4:00 P.M. This leg proved one of the easiest to navigate thanks to numerous railroads, rivers and mountains, but the fliers encountered severe rain squalls, a preview of the monsoon season, which was just building. Amelia would have to fly the Electra southeast, directly into the fierce monsoon winds and their heavy, driving rains.

The next morning, weather forecasters gave AE a choice of evils. It had rained all night and the field was already thoroughly soaked, making takeoff a precarious affair. However, more rain was coming. Earhart could either try to fly through it, with a chance of dodging the major squalls, or stay to wait it out and most likely get stuck when the field became waterlogged. Time was pressing her toward Oakland and the Fourth of July celebrations GP was planning. She decided to get airborne right away.

It seemed that Amelia was plagued by devils on all sides—GP in the States, Noonan with his bottle, the mud of India. Those, and more, were always pushing and pushing. And the ones within? They pushed the hardest.

As Amelia remembered, "That takeoff was precarious, perhaps as risky as any we had. The plane clung for what seemed like ages to the heavy sticky soil before the wheels finally lifted, and we cleared with nothing at all to spare the fringe of trees at the airdrome's edge."

Then they pressed on for Akyab, Burma, to refuel at the excellent airport where Imperial Airways, Air France and KLM stopped regularly. After a quick turnaround, AE and Fred took off for Rangoon in spite of a grim weather forecast. Before long the Electra was caught in rough air and relentless rain. "The monsoon, I find, lets down more liquid per second than I thought could come out of the skies. Everything was obliterated in the deluge, so savage that it beat off patches of paint along the leading edge of my plane's wings. Only a flying submarine could have prospered."

After trying to penetrate "an almost unbroken wall of water" for a couple of hours, Amelia gave up and turned back to try to find Akyab. Visibility was down to a few hundred yards, forcing her to fly out to sea and let down just over the surface. In spite of the friction between the crew, Amelia appreciated Noonan when his talents came to the fore. "By uncanny powers, Fred Noonan managed to navigate us back to the airport, without being able to see anything but the waves beneath our plane."

Gladly down at Akyab again, Amelia was told that the conditions she encountered were normal and could be expected to last for three months. Regardless, she and Fred tried twice more that day to get through, each time coming back to their starting point exhausted and defeated. After waiting a day, they were off again on June 19 with the hope of reaching Bangkok. The weather was even worse than the day before, but using their new hedge-hopping technique they hoped to "sneak underneath the monsoon." Visibility eventually went down to zero. Fearing collision with the ground, Amelia climbed on instruments to 8000 feet, crossed the mountains and barged through.

Reaching Rangoon, having covered a mere 400 miles, AE decided to land. Only minutes after they taxied in, the rain poured down so heavily that a takeoff for Bangkok would have been hazardous. The Electra would have to stay put for the time being. As the guest of the American consul, Austin C. Brady, the two fliers enjoyed their forced stay by touring the famous city.

The next morning the pair struck out for Siam, still fighting the murderous rains. Once the mountains separating Burma and Siam were crossed, the clouds broke and AE brought the aircraft down toward Bangkok. After another quick refueling they departed for Singapore, 900 miles away, in sparkling weather.

But another demon was raising its head. It was obvious that Noonan was becoming weary of the constant fight with bad weather. It was reflected when, speaking of the clear skies on the way to Singapore, he said, "I thought there was no more weather like this"—it was as if he had given up ever flying in good weather again. Noonan was a world-class navigator and should not have been affected by the weather. His fatigue was starting to show.

Now, with everything going so well, Amelia was determined to reach Singapore. And at 5:25 that afternoon Amelia and Noonan touched down on the almost endlessly stretching runway at the new $9 million airport there.

Amelia and Fred had been a source of amusement or disappointment for their hosts around the world, depending upon their temperament. When Singapore's American consul general, Monnett B. Davis, and his wife offered their hospitality to the sojourners, Amelia was pleased "they had courage enough to take us for the night, even after I explained our disagreeable habit of getting up at three in the morning and falling asleep immediately after dinner."

Early on June 21 the pair set course for Java, passing over the open sea, then along the westerly shores of Sumatra. During the first hour out they crossed the equator for the third time. Above the volcanic mountains of Java, they were joined and led by military aircraft to Bandoeng, "perched among densely wooded mountains," where they landed. An hour after their arrival another phone call from GP in New York reached Amelia. She was awed and delighted that modern technology would allow a conversation to be held with someone half a world away.

While at Bandoeng, they set aside at least two days for the local arm of KLM to work on the Electra. This gave AE one of her few chances during the trip to enjoy a foreign country. One interestng venture in Java was an inspection trip to a local volcano, which had last erupted in 1910. Amelia was duly impressed with the yellow-white hissing steam blowing from the crevices of the pit at 6500 feet above sea level.

At 3:45 A.M. on June 24 Amelia was warming up the Electra's engines, preparing to fly all the way to Australia. Going through her preflight checks, she found that one instrument would not function. Soon everyone with an idea about what might be wrong took a crack at fixing it. It was not until 2:00 P.M. "that the distemper was sufficiently cured to warrant proceeding." As the sun was setting, the Lockheed landed at Saurabaya, 350 miles away, and the "faulty long-distance flying instruments" (which she did not identify) were still in need of repair. The next morning, greatly discouraged, she flew back to Bandoeng so the Dutch mechanics could get things working again.

With more time to kill, Amelia continued to enjoy the wonderful hospitality and culture surrounding her. Fred, on the other hand, was not bearing up well under the strain of Amelia's aggressive schedule. Ever since South America he had been increasingly falling back on his old habit for comfort.

By the evening of June 26 it looked as if the Electra was back in top form. AE placed what would be her last phone call to GP, who was in Cheyenne, Wyoming, en route to California, while his United airliner was being refueled. According to Putnam's close friend and colleague, Van Campen Heilner, Amelia was relieved to catch George. She started the conversation with the remark, "He's hitting the bottle again and I don't even know where he's getting it!" Though the whole conversation was recorded, Putnam included only the last portion concerning the Lockheed in *Last Flight.*

G.P.P.—"Is everything about the ship O.K. now?"
A.E.—"Yes. Good night, Hon."
G.P.P.—"Good night. . . . I'll be sitting in Oakland waiting for you."

Amelia Earhart, whose faith in Fred Noonan was wearing thin, now faced the possibility of having to do more of the navigation on her own even though her navigator was aboard.

At Howland Island preparations were completed for the Electra's arrival. The runways were ready and the government officials stayed busy scaring off the numerous sea birds. On the twenty-fourth a party from the *Itasca* landed to set up the experimental DF while the *Ontario* stationed itself at sea between Lae and Howland to give midpoint contact if possible.

Finally, on Sunday, June 27, Amelia and Fred left Bandoeng for Port Darwin, Australia, aware that hours of daylight would be lost the further east they flew. Five hours out, the Lockheed landed at Koepang on the island of Timor without enough time to refuel and make Australia by sunset.

There were no facilities on the airfield, which was surrounded by a stone fence to keep out wild pigs, except a small fuel-storage shed. The Electra was staked down for the night with engine and propeller covers attached. Amelia used the remainder of the day for sightseeing; then she and Fred were given quarters at the Rest House.

Early the next morning they set off across the Timor Sea, bucking strong headwinds at 7000 feet. Australia finally stretched out in front of the Electra as a vast plain, and AE descended for Port Darwin on the northern coast. "We were pounced upon by a doctor as we rolled to a stop, and thereupon were examined thoroughly for tropical disease. No one could approach us or the airplane until we had passed muster," which took ten hours. The delay centered around the smallpox certificate they presented, which had been signed by a private American doctor instead of a public health official as required by the Australians. Though the Electra had to clear customs as if it were an ocean-going vessel, this formality was dispensed with as much as possible in light of the extended quarantine.

When AE was asked why she had not used the field's radio direction-finding facilities, she told the officials that her DF was not working. Army Sergeant Stan Rose checked it over and found a fuse had blown, which he replaced. A test of the set proved it to be in good order, and Amelia was advised to check the fuse first should the DF malfunction again.

–On June 29 Amelia and Fred took off at 6:29 A.M. for Lae, New Guinea. About two thirds of the leg was over water dotted with small islands. AE "had been told the clouds often hang low over this region and it was better to climb above its hazardous minarets than to run the risks of dodging them should we lay our course close to the surface." They also had to clear the Owen Stanley Mountains, which stretched the length of New Guinea between Port Moresby and Lae.

— After 1200 miles, flown in 7 hours and 43 minutes, the Electra touched down on the 3000-foot strip at Lae. The next leg, to Howland Island, would be the most challenging and the most dangerous of the flight.

Amelia Earhart and Fred Noonan were about to meet their demons face to face as the whole world watched and waited.

Chapter 5

Search

Vince Loomis: 1967–1985

*A*FTER my 1952 Air Force tour in the Marshalls, I gave little thought to what had taken place there. It had been another in a long series of service assignments carried out in obedience to orders. My memories of my Micronesian experiences lay dormant for fifteen years until, in 1967, I happened to pick up a magazine during a flight from Eglin Air Force Base, Florida, to California.

In the pages of *Reader's Digest* I came across a condensation of Fred Goerner's book *The Search for Amelia Earhart*. A CBS newsman, Goerner was one of the many who had caught what he termed "Earhart fever"—a compulsion to find out what had really happened to the famous aviatrix. I was enthralled with each page as I read of his investigation into her disappearance. Goerner came to the conclusion that Earhart and Noonan had been on a spy mission for the U.S. government, overflying islands being fortified for war. He firmly believed that they had been captured by the Japanese and imprisoned on Saipan, where they died.

I was fascinated with the idea. What if the Electra had not fallen into the ocean near Howland Island? How much fuel would have been left for it to land elsewhere? Could Earhart have made it to another of the tiny specks that dot the Pacific and crash-landed?

These random thoughts made their way through my mind as I sat looking out across the sky from my airplane seat. Then I was jolted as a memory flashed through my mind . . . the aircraft my Air Force team had stumbled across in 1952. Someone had mentioned the possibility it belonged to Earhart. Had we come upon the lost Electra? The more I pondered, the more fantastic the idea seemed. How could Earhart have gotten so far off course? If she did end up in Saipan, the Marshall Islands were certainly out of the way.

I tried, without much luck, to recall what the wreckage had looked like. Not only had it been covered with thick greenery, but fifteen years back I hadn't been interested in anything but getting my job done. The details were so dim that I could not even remember upon which of the many atolls the aircraft lay.

Though I did not have much time or money to investigate Amelia's disappearance, I decided to begin a modest effort that week in 1967. I had nothing to start with except a wrecked airplane, so I began with the end result—how would the Electra have ended up on an atoll in the Marshall Islands? As an Air Force pilot and navigator in the Pacific, familiar with long-distance over-ocean flying, I felt I had a start.

By the mid-1970s I was spending all of my spare time researching the mystery, delving into each of the theories that had been put forth since 1937. Though I thought an examination of the work done by previous searchers would be a help, I let myself in for one long roller-coaster ride to the heights of lunacy and the depths of incredulity.

Expecting work that was substantiated by credible research, I found full-blown theories drawn out of the smallest premises. In spite of a number of "eyewitness" reports of what happened to Amelia, none of the theories were substantiated by supporting evidence, and on the whole they were contradictory. What I had come up with among the host of hunters who had caught "Earhart fever" was a series of amazing stories. To sort through the maze was a frustrating and time-consuming experience.

Amelia Earhart Lives—Joe Klaas put this fantastic theory before the public in 1970 in a book of that title. Working with Joe Gervais, who had conducted his own research called "Operation Earhart," Klaas asserted that a woman named Irene Bolam, living in New Jersey, was Amelia Earhart. As if that were not incredible enough, Klaas and Gervais claimed to have located Fred Noonan, also living under another name. Though both people looked somewhat like the famous pair, they vehemently denied any connection.

Gervais's theory had Earhart overflying Truk and the Mar-

shalls, then planning to get "lost" intentionally by landing on
Canton Island so the Navy could search the Japanese mandated
islands. This scenario was almost identical to a Rosalind Russell
movie of 1943, *Flight for Freedom*, in which the heroine, closely
modeled on Earhart, was to land on "Gull Island."

However, according to Klaas, something went wrong and the
Japanese forced the Electra down on Hull Island (this name was
so close to the movie island's, it was ridiculous) and captured
Earhart. She was taken to Japan, where she spent World War II
as a prisoner in the Imperial Palace. Her release was obtained in
exchange for U.S. promises that the emperor would not be tried
as a war criminal and would remain head of state. Upon returning
to America, both Earhart and Noonan were sworn to secrecy.
The book also intimated that the Electra made it back to America
listed as a similar Lockheed 12A Electra Junior. It carried the
same registration number, NR16020, and crashed into a mountain and burned in 1961.

Gervais finally met Bolam in 1965. She was wearing a minia-
ture major's oak-leaf insignia and an enameled replica of the red,
white and blue ribbon representing the Distinguished Flying
Cross (both of which Earhart would have been entitled to wear).
Gervais tried to see her again in Montreal, but they missed con-
nections. He then telephoned her. She asked him why he wanted
to see her, and he explained that if you put the names of the eight
Phoenix Islands in a certain order and then crossed out certain
letters, the name of her husband showed up—and that, furthermore, the numerical sequence of the letters in his name reproduced the exact longitude and latitude of Hull Island!

That this jumbled logic was ever printed as serious research
gives some idea of how far people will go to prove their theories.
Federal Aviation Administration records have shown the crashed
aircraft to be Paul Mantz's Lockheed 12, renumbered in honor of
Amelia. No evidence has been unearthed concerning Earhart's
supposed stay in the Imperial Palace. Yet, to this day, the authors
affirm that they are correct.

Another man, ex–World War II Marine Thom Thomas, published a book claiming that after the Japanese surrender in 1945
he saw Amelia working as a prostitute for the Japanese fisherman
who had rescued her from the ditched Electra near Howland Is-

land. Thomas did not question the fisherman after paying for the services of the white woman, who he asserted had amnesia because she could not answer any questions about how she had arrived in Japan. His basis for determining that the white slave was Earhart boiled down to her resemblance to the famous flyer. Though he later went back to Japan to find Earhart in the small fishing village he had visited, predictably there was no trace of her.

Theories claiming that Amelia had survived the crash of the Electra were not new by any means. Beginning the day the aircraft vanished, there were reports from ship radio rooms, military and commercial stations, radio amateurs and airline radio personnel claiming to have heard Amelia's call letters, KHAQQ, in code or by voice on 3105 and 6210 kilocycles, Earhart's radio frequencies. Some reports were quite definite in stating Earhart had transmitted clearly that she was on a Pacific island or afloat at sea.

Pan Am's radio stations at Makapuu Point, Hawaii, and Wake Island took bearings on nondescript transmissions that seemed to be coming from somewhere in the Phoenix Islands south-southeast of Howland. The direction finder on Howland picked up a continuous wave of unknown origin on 3105 kilocycles indicating a heading south-southeast or north-northwest from the island.

Though none of these transmissions were proved to have come from the Electra, rumors began to circulate that Earhart was in communication with numerous stations after her last transmission to the *Itasca*. The Coast Guard tried to put these rumors to rest in March 1938 by stating, "*Not one* of the amateur [radio] reports received during the Earhart search was accurate, and all reports of receipt of signals from the Earhart plane were definitely known to be false." Yet numerous Earhart theorists continue to use the bearings in an attempt to locate the Electra.

George Putnam had Amelia declared legally dead on January 5, 1939. In December of the same year *Popular Aviation* published an article entitled "Is Amelia Earhart Still Alive?," raising the question why a declaration of death should have been made five and a half years before the legal time limit of seven years. Another article, "The War's First Casualty," appeared in the November 1942 issue of *Skyways*. Author Charles Palmer felt there were "irresistibly irregular" aspects surrounding the flight. Could the Japanese have discovered a scheme to overfly the mandated islands? Had the Navy used its search for the Electra to get a look at Japanese fortifications? Why did the U.S. government build airstrips and station ships as plane guards for the private flight? Why had Earhart refused to radio her position to the *Itasca*?

The possibility that Amelia had been a government spy found a new school of believers, who began to piece a number of irregularities into apparently logical progression to prove the point.

Hollywood saw the potential of inflating the story for wartime movie audiences ready to hear about brave Americans who had known what the Japanese were up to when the rest of the country was asleep. In April 1943 RKO released *Flight for Freedom*, starring Rosalind Russell and Fred MacMurray, a thinly veiled reconstruction of Earhart's last flight. Even the minor details of the round-the-world journey were reproduced. However, to avoid direct mention of plane or crew, names were changed and the aircraft was marked NR16055 instead of the real NR16020. This film served as inspiration for Klaas, Gervais and several other theorists.

The government-spy theory received a tremendous boost in 1948, when Amelia's mother, Amy, stated she knew her daughter had been on a secret mission under the direction of President Franklin D. Roosevelt. Though many opinions were put forth concerning the possibility of government involvement, there were no confirmations.

The closest anyone came to resolving the question at the time was Amelia's friend and fellow aviatrix Jacqueline Cochran. Jackie made a special postwar trip to Japan under orders from U.S. Army Air Force Commanding General Henry H. "Hap" Arnold to investigate a number of items, among them Earhart's disappearance. Though she reported discovering files dealing with Earhart, they were never made public and no one has found them since. This later fueled a host of theories claiming that the government was involved in a massive cover-up of the truth about the Electra's disappearance, "proving" by omission that Earhart was on a secret spy mission.

In 1960 the Earhart theorists were given a new area for conjecture when Josephine Blanco Akiyama, a Saipanese native, said she had seen an American white woman on her home island in 1937. Both the woman and a male companion were in the custody of the Japanese. Though she had been very young at the time, Miss Blanco identified the woman as looking much like Earhart. Several military personnel who had served on Saipan during World War II had heard stories that Earhart was imprisoned there, but Blanco was the first native to make a public statement. Her story was later repeated in detail in Paul Briand, Jr.'s, biography of Earhart, *Daughter of the Sky.*

As Blanco's story was circulated, a host of contradictory theories emerged to explain how Earhart could have arrived on Saipan. Thomas E. Devine, a technical sergeant on Saipan in early July 1944, claimed to have seen a twin-engine, twin-tail airplane with the number NR16020 painted on it. He said that Marines guarding the plane at Aslito Airfield stated it had belonged to Earhart. The plane was said to have been destroyed shortly thereafter in an explosion and subsequent fire.

About a year later Devine, standing near a cemetery on Saipan, was told by a native woman that two white people, a man and a woman who had come from the sky, were buried in the graveyard. When the Earhart disappearance came into the public eye again, Devine began his own investigations into what might have happened. He returned to Saipan several times to talk with those who remembered the story. The U.S. government supposedly closed several doors to his investigation, and Devine heard of documents on Earhart that had "disappeared." This confusion convinced Devine there was indeed a cover-up. Finally Devine concluded that Noonan, upon locating the Electra's position on a sun line 157°–337° and being unable to find Howland Island, had navigated the plane for Guam, the nearest and largest U.S. territory. Through mistake or plan, the Lockheed, he believed, actually landed on Japanese-held Saipan, only 115 miles north.

Josephine Blanco's story launched Fred Goerner's search for Amelia as well. He made four trips to Saipan, some with Devine, and traveled all over the United States interviewing people and hunting for records. With the help of the Catholic priests on Saipan, Goerner interviewed several people, some of whom had seen people closely resembling Earhart and Noonan in 1937. These natives were sure the two Americans had been executed or had died of disease.

Goerner theorized in his 1966 book that the Electra had been on a secret intelligence mission to overfly Truk, the major Japanese bastion in the Pacific. Though much was made of the Electra's having secret engine changes for more powerful motors, special camera installations and special spy gear, none of these modifications were confirmed. Not only would the Electra have been far short of fuel for such a mission, but the aircraft would have been over the "target" in the middle of the night when cameras would be useless; there was no infrared equipment in those days, and use of photoflash would have given Earhart away immediately.

Though most of Goerner's research efforts ended in conjecture without substantiating evidence, clearly the Saipanese remembered seeing captured white people before the war. How could the two fliers have made it all the way to Saipan, when the Electra would have run out of fuel far short?

As the Earhart disappearance continued to make news in the 1960s, still other servicemen reported seeing photographs taken from Japanese prisoners on Saipan in 1944 that showed Earhart in front of a Japanese aircraft or with a Japanese soldier. In 1944, Marines Everett Hensen and Billy Burks had dug up a grave just outside Garapan City and found two skeletons. When they asked the officer in command, a Captain Griswold, about the grave, he reportedly replied, "Have you ever heard of Amelia Earhart?"— and told the men to say nothing. That they had said nothing for over twenty years amazed me, particularly with all the attention the mystery had received in the late 1940s.

Joe Davidson told of yet another discovery on Saipan in a book he wrote in 1969, entitled *Amelia Earhart Returns from Saipan*. That book tells about two trips made to the area in 1967 and 1968 by an expedition from Cleveland. One of the members of the expedition, Donald Kothera, claimed to have seen a twin-engine airplane in a box canyon in 1946. He said the plane was undamaged but had no engines; therefore he didn't think it could have landed there.

During the first trip the group located the canyon but only

found a few parts of the aircraft. These were analyzed, and it was found that the aluminum used in the airplane had been produced by Alcoa before 1937. On their second trip they interviewed people who said they knew of the aircraft or had seen AE or Fred Noonan.

As others had found in previous investigations, the American flyers were remembered by several Saipanese, in particular Anna Magofa, who had been seven years old in 1937. She told of seeing two Japanese guarding a white man and woman who were digging a hole just outside the cemetery near Garapan City. The man, she said, was blindfolded and then beheaded. She couldn't forget what she had seen for years, and even had nightmares about it. She always thought that the tall·white man with the big nose seemed much nicer than the Japanese propagandists had wanted her to believe.

Magofa took the Cleveland group to where she said the execution had taken place, and there they found a three-tooth gold dental bridge and some bone fragments. It seemed to the group that the grave had been dug up before. An anthropologist later determined that the bones were "those of a female, probably white individual, between the anatomical ages of forty and forty-two"—and also that one of the bones belonged to the "remains of a second individual, a male."

When the group made inquiries of official U.S. agencies, the State Department is supposed to have admitted having a classified file on Earhart but did not release it. The group's conclusion was that top civil and military authorities had much to do with Earhart prior to her last flight and that there was a need for officials in high places to come forward with the full story.

Reports from more servicemen surfaced, this time those who had been in the Marshall Islands after the 1944 invasion. They told of natives who had seen a white lady pilot and a white man captured by the Japanese after their plane came down. A Marine described finding a barracks room fitted out for a woman. It contained a suitcase, inside which were some clippings about Earhart, clothing and a locked diary entitled "10-Year Diary of Amelia Earhart." Natives told another Marine that they remembered a white woman and a white man near Kwajalein in 1937, who were then taken to another island.

* * *

What a mass of confusion. Not only Saipan, but the Marshalls, where I had seen the wreck, Truk, Guam, Hull Island, the other Phoenix Islands or an ocean ditching near Howland were being mentioned as the final resting place for plane and/or crew. How could Earhart have been seen in so many places? Clearly not all of the contradictory suppositions were true. I could easily lead myself down any one of many paths that would end up nowhere.

The heart of several of these theories lay with secret government documents or revelations. Conveniently, nothing was forthcoming from official agencies, so each theorist was free to draw his own conclusions without evidence. However, I could not ignore the body of testimony from the Saipanese and, to a much smaller extent, a few Marshallese. These people provided the only potential eyewitness accounts of what might have happened. Though Saipan had been visited numerous times by investigators, no one had gone to the Marshalls to ask the same questions. I had been there once. Maybe I could go again and retrace my steps, interviewing as many natives as possible.

I was left with a wide gulf to span between the crashed airplane I had seen in the Marshalls and the claimed eyewitnesses. Possibly these natives were out to make some money. Who knew if what they were saying could be relied upon? If I was going to get anywhere at all, I would have to find hard evidence, which so many had failed to find. If the wreck I remembered could be located and proved to be the Electra (a truly slim possibility), that would solve the mystery of where it came down, but what about the Americans' subsequent fate? If the Japanese had captured them, surely someone had to be left who remembered.

Though I had read through the host of theories with some hope of a solution, I was now farther away than ever. The real story was still unknown. If I was going to find anything new, clearly it would take a great deal of effort.

Where to start? How could the Electra have ended up in the Marshalls after being close to Howland Island when Earhart was last heard? If I started with the final resting place of the aircraft and worked backward, instead of beginning with Lae as all the other searchers had, maybe I could find out. My first move would be a trip to the Marshall Islands to locate the aircraft.

Though State Department red tape was impressively hard to cut, my wife, Georgie, and I obtained the necessary visas and left for Majuro, the urban center of Marshallese society, in April 1978. The small atolls I had visited in 1952 were several hundred miles away from Majuro, but this was the only place where I could contact island officials and then try to find a ship that could take us where we needed to go. This sounded simple, but it was a tall order, for I could not remember upon which of the many islands the aircraft was located. I would have to visit the entire chain of northern atolls and their numerous islands individually.

Inbound to Majuro on the airliner, I overheard a discussion between Senator Amata Kabua and Tony DeBrum, chairman and vice chairman, respectively, of the Marshall Islands Political Status Commission seeking independence from the United States. After introducing myself and finding out that the senator was a direct descendant of Kabua the Great, the first king of the Marshalls, I told them my reason for visiting the islands. Without hesitation Kabua said that he believed Earhart had come down in the islands and that her aircraft was still there! DeBrum was even more emphatic: "We all know about this woman who was reported to have come down on Mili southeast of Majuro, was captured by the Japanese and taken off to Jaluit. I believe this is exactly what happened. Remember, the stories were being told long before you Americans began asking questions."

I was so surprised that I found it hard to talk. Here I was on the way to try to find an old airplane, and two natives matter-of-factly said they knew just what had happened. Why had no one ever reported what the Marshallese believed? Certainly it was a lead, even though it was hearsay and might not be true. Apparently Saipan had captured all the attention; Kabua and DeBrum said the story had been told for years among the Marshallese, but very few outsiders stayed long enough to listen.

DeBrum suggested that when I got settled on Majuro I look up a few of those who might have seen something first-hand. It was that simple. The two Marshallese did not appear the least concerned with my astonishment, but they were friendly and offered to help during my stay. For the remainder of the flight I was in a daze.

After getting settled at the hotel, we met American Ben Barry, who had made the islands his home. He not only became a good friend but was most helpful in getting us around while giving us a complete rundown on those things we needed to know to avoid social blunders and taboos.

The third morning after our arrival we had breakfast with Senator Kabua, still referred to by the people as Iroij, or king, because of his royal blood. A number of islanders came up to pay their respects to him; they would bow or even get down on their knees. We were introduced to several people, among them Steve, brother of the chief on Wotho, one of the atolls I had visited in 1952. Much to my pleasure, he remembered my putting a canvas panel on the atoll twenty-six years earlier, but he recalled nothing of an airplane.

Though the Marshallese as a whole were not prone to tell things freely to outsiders, with the senator's blessings placed upon us at that meal we were able to seek out others who had heard the story of the "lady pilot." I had come to find an airplane and had stumbled upon some leads I could not ignore. But it turned out that getting a boat to take us the hundreds of miles over open ocean to the northern atolls was impossible. And there were no aircraft available other than the airliner to Kwajalein, still a major U.S. military installation since its capture from the Japanese in 1944.

The Marshallese we visited over the next few days had not actually seen an American plane or crew before the war. However, they mentioned hearing from Japanese friends of a lady pilot landing near Mili Atoll, a few hundred miles away. Elieu Jibambam, Henry Mueller and Mark Judah had heard the Japanese tell the story, and Elieu had mentioned this to U.S. Navy Lieutenant Gene Bogan, who was stationed in the islands after they were captured.

Elieu told Bogan that one of his Japanese friends, Ajima, a South Seas trader, heard of a lady pilot who came down near Mili before the war and was picked up by a fishing boat and taken to Jaluit, the Japanese headquarters in the Marshalls, then to Saipan. Elieu had been fearful of telling the story and withheld it until the Marshalls were firmly in American hands in 1944. "Nobody know I can speak English. What I tell you is what I heard and believe true. It was too dangerous for me and my friend to talk. When Gene Bogan came to the island, I work for him and help him catch six Japanese. He is the first one I tell the story to."

Though Bogan made a report of Elieu's story to his superiors, apparently it was ignored; at least, it was never followed up. Shortly thereafter, Japan surrendered and Bogan returned to the States.

The story was like a shot of adrenaline to me, but it was still third-hand. If there was any truth to it at all, there had to be eyewitnesses who would talk. Much to my frustration, I could not find them before leaving. Heading for home at 30,000 feet, I resolved to come back. If I could find the aircraft, all the better, but regardless, I was going to hunt down the Marshallese who claimed to have seen something first-hand.

I headed back to Majuro in July 1979 with several people serving as photographers and assistants. If we never found the wreck I had seen, we could still very well uncover the truth.

My first meeting was with the former senator, now newly elected president, Kabua. Without hesitation he gave us permission to visit Mili, the atoll mentioned by the Marshallese as the crash site, to search for artifacts and interview witnesses. However, we would also have to obtain permission from the atoll's landowners themselves and then arrange for small boats to take us over the couple of hundred miles of open sea. From the comments made to us, I gathered the journey was not without some risk, and I have to admit I did not look forward to crossing the ocean in a tiny boat.

Word we were back made its way around Majuro, and before long people were willing to talk with us. One woman described living on Jaluit before the war, where she saw a white man beheaded—though she could not speak English, she drew her hand across her throat when talking of the Japanese form of execution. The Marshallese were often called out by their Oriental masters to dig graves, where prisoners were made to kneel. The natives would then be forced to witness the beheadings and fill in the graves.

The woman remembered that the Japanese became very strict

after 1936 and beheaded people for little or no reason. Only Japanese reading material was allowed for the islanders; if books in other languages were found, the punishment could be execution. As a result, the Marshallese buried their "foreign" books in secret places. When asked if she recalled what happened to the white man who had come down with the lady pilot, she said she thought he had been beheaded on Jaluit.

More hearsay. To be so close to what seemed the truth and not get it first-hand was unnerving. I got more of the same when interviewing Kurt Pinho, a Portuguese native who had settled in the islands. He had heard the Earhart story often from those he knew, the details always the same. She had come down on Mili, was taken prisoner and transferred to Jaluit, finally dying on Saipan. He mentioned a Mili resident, Anibar Eini, who as a boy had been a witness to the crash. After the Japanese picked up the aircraft, Anibar dived to a wing that had broken off. Apparently it had stayed in the water all these years. Kurt also mentioned how easy it had been for the Japanese to dominate the passive Marshallese, who were happy to trade labor for food in spite of the often harsh discipline.

The stories were certainly interesting; they pointed out the attitude of the Japanese and how they dominated the islands. Had Earhart come down in the Marshalls, she and Noonan would have had a hard time explaining what they were doing there.

One of the more tantalizing interviews was with Dr. John, a retired businessman on Majuro who owned a number of stores near the airport and also practiced medicine. When we asked him about an American lady pilot and an airplane going down on Mili, his home atoll, he stated very simply that he had seen an aircraft go down in the water about 200 feet offshore on one of the islands but that he did not see its crew. I have to admit my heart skipped a beat—had we found an eyewitness? He was not certain what happened after that, for discussion of the subject had not been allowed by the Japanese. Dr. John could not elaborate; that was all he saw. He assured us that there were other witnesses living on Mili who had seen more. I was ready to leave that minute, but the Marshallese are in no hurry to go anywhere, so I had to bide my time until our boats were rented.

Though we could not find a way to the northern islands and

the wrecked airplane I remembered, with permission from the landowners on Mili I obtained three boats to visit their atoll in order to interview eyewitnesses and, if at all possible, find some of the Electra. I did not know why it would have gone down at the opposite end of the island chain from where I had seen a wreck many years before, but I wasn't about to let the leads pointing to Mili go unexplored.

We sailed over some rough seas, and by morning we had entered the northern channel entrance to Mili Atoll. The islanders came out of their thatched huts; children ran playfully up and down the shore. Elgin Daniel, the chief magistrate of Mili, who had accompanied us from Majuro after attending to some business, went ashore first to explain our reason for being there. As our dinghy went in next, it was met by the only power-driven boat on the atoll. About twenty feet long, it had an old gasoline engine in the middle held together with wire, coconut vines and whatever else would keep it working. It roared along at a top speed of less than five knots, and when the throttle was used, great plumes of smoke would puff from all over the engine, which would backfire. The vessel was known as Mili's "Boom-Boom Navy."

The first to greet us was a young resident, Gideon Dominic, who spoke excellent English. A native of the Gilbert Islands who now lived in the Marshalls, he offered to help us during our stay before returning to his home islands to marry a girl he had never met. (Contract marriage, arranged by parents, is still a strong institution in Micronesia.) Dominic became one of our most valuable team members, particularly as an interpreter of both the language and the customs.

Nothing could have prepared us for what followed. With a flurry of activity the queen of Mili, Bosket Diklan, arrived. This warm, smiling giant of a woman with a booming voice welcomed each member of the expedition by chanting, placing a lei around the neck, and tapping each side of the head, which she grabbed while pumping her arms up and down, bobbing the head toward her bosom and still singing the chant. She was quite strong and my head literally rang, but the ceremony was full of joy and great fun. It gave us the freedom of her lands, something we much appreciated, and it also opened the way for an interview with Her Majesty.

Bosket had been married to Takinami, the Japanese commanding officer and South Seas Trading Company representative on Mili before the war. I sat down with her and told her we were hoping she could remember something about the lady pilot who had crashed on Mili. She replied she knew about her. She had come down on the ocean side of the atoll on a coral reef. Bosket had seen the aircraft itself but not the crew—"The Japanese didn't want us to see anything." Immediately after the lady pilot's plane came down, Takinami was called to Jaluit, but Bosket was not told what happened. He was later reassigned to Japan, and she never saw him again. She also recalled that Jaluit had been a center for Japanese imprisonment.

I am sure I must have looked dumbfounded as the queen told her story. So glibly she had stated she had seen the plane. Was she sure? Could it have been another aircraft that came down during the war and not the Electra? No, she was quite sure of what she had said, but knew nothing more. That was the end of the interview, and it was made clear we could leave the hut.

Still trying to digest what we had heard, from there we went to interview our boat navigator's wife, who according to Mili natives had also seen a plane come down before the war. Clement had done a fine job of guiding us through the waters of Mili Atoll, and he seemed to be open to our search for information. However, with our first question Clement jumped in and refused to let his wife talk. Every time she opened her mouth, he silenced her and answered the questions himself, although he had been away on Jaluit at the time of Amelia's landing. He knew all about it, but from hearsay. We packed up our gear and left.

Later I was able to get a few words with his wife alone. "Clement knows nothing," she said. "I tell you I saw this airplane and the woman pilot and the Japanese taking the woman and the man with her away. I don't know why he won't let me speak. I think he wants vodka first." We were a bit short on alcohol, since it was not allowed in the outer islands. I asked her where she saw the plane. She pointed and said, "Over there . . . next to Barre Island. That's where it landed."

With that our conversation ended. What next? Did I have a real eyewitness here or just another storyteller? If she had really seen what she related, then we had made a major breakthrough. Extreme frustration mixed with elation fails to describe the swings of emotion I was feeling. How could I be so close and yet so far? Before we left, I was going to do everything in my power to visit Barre Island.

We left Mili Mili, the major island of Mili Atoll, the next morning with two boats, first for Alu Island to talk with Jororo Alibar and Anibar Eini, Mili fishermen who had been recommended to me as eyewitnesses to the crash. I waded ashore at Alu with David, President Kabua's son, who had offered to be one of our guides, through three-foot-deep water on top of sharp coral. Though I had boots on, the small bits worked their way under my toenails, and my feet were bleeding by the time I had struggled the half mile to the beach.

Jororo wasn't home—he had taken his outrigger to visit a friend and go fishing five islands away. However, Anibar was on the island. This slightly built, elderly man finally arrived to meet with us, but he appeared to be suspicious of our purposes. He did not return our smile of greeting. When David asked about the lady pilot, Anibar said he remembered nothing. Yet he had told many others of seeing the aircraft ditch and of diving down to one of its severed wings. This man was not interested in how far I had come or how much trouble it had been to get to him. Looking around at Anibar's friends, I got the same treatment—they offered nothing but stares.

I was more than disappointed. Why couldn't these people say more? Were they afraid of us? Mad at our intrusion into their islands? Did memories of the Japanese still have some sort of hold on them? We headed back for the boat across that half mile of coral. Once aboard, we set off for Ejowa, where we found Jororo's outrigger bobbing up and down in the water. Another trek over the coral with my black leather boots scooped up increasing amounts of coral. By the time we found Jororo, I was in extreme pain.

This Marshallese fisherman showed some signs of hard times. He was missing a foot and several fingers as a result of American bombing attacks. Understandably he had no love for us; he was pro-Japanese. When asked if he remembered his friend Lijon, who we were told had seen the crash as well, he asked, David interpreted, how we had come to him to ask about the lady pilot. How had he heard what we were after? These people obviously shared their news rapidly—it must have been a form of entertainment.

I explained we had heard of him from Ralph Middle, a member of the war reparations group that had traveled through the islands to assess Japanese damage. Ralph told us before we left Majuro that he had talked with two Mili fishermen, Jororo Alibar and his friend Lijon, about what the Japanese had done before and during the war. Only after Middle had spent several days with them did he gain their confidence enough to have them talk freely with him.

As the three were relaxing together, one of the Marshallese offhandedly mentioned they had seen an airplane crash in the water before the war. That did not strike Middle as particularly unusual until the crew was described—they were white, and one was a woman. Middle related the story told by Jororo and Lijon.

> It was sometime before the war that they saw an airplane land on the reef about 200 feet offshore. They said they were very frightened and hid in the jungle, then remained hidden while what they thought were two men got out of the plane into a yellow boat and came ashore. It was shortly after they got on the island that the fishermen saw them bury a silver container. Shortly thereafter, the Japanese arrived and started to question the two flyers, one of whom was taller than the other.
>
> During the questioning the Japanese started to slap the flyers, at which time one of them started to scream. At that point they realized one was a woman. They stayed hidden because they knew the Japanese would have killed them for what they had witnessed.

(The story of the "silver container" was certainly plausible. Later, when reading Earhart's *Last Flight*, I discovered Fred Noonan had carried a tin box aboard the Electra with him before taking off from Lae for Howland. Paul Rafford, a former Pan Am employee whom I met later, wondered if the rattle inside the container revealed a bottle of alcohol.)

Jororo replied that he knew about the lady pilot and the plane crash, but did not see a metal box that was buried. He said Lijon had known of the box, which was buried under a *Kanal* tree, but that he had not been with Lijon when he saw it, and Lijon was now dead.

Confronted with his report to Middle, Jororo said it had been a long time ago, and then contradicted his latest account by saying he didn't remember after all. How in the world was I going to tie all this together? I feared I was not going to get any cooperation. Though I knew money meant little to the islanders, I thought I'd give it a try. "Tell him we're offering two thousand dollars to anyone who can help us find the metal box." The fisherman smiled the smile of a man who had no need of money. I asked if he knew where the plane went down. When he said he did, I got out a map of Mili. He quickly pointed out the reef adjacent to Barre and Bokonariowa islands. He said part of the plane was still there. I didn't understand why he was sharing this with us, but Barre had also been mentioned by Clement's wife as the spot where she had seen the aircraft go down. In spite of the maze I was wandering through at times, at least a few facts were surfacing that I could investigate.

We sailed for Barre, and after coming ashore, I had the search party split up. One group was to look for the wing Anibar had told others of seeing after the crash, while Dominic and I tried to locate the *Kanal* tree under which the container was buried. Our two metal detectors turned out to be very ineffective, and there must have been dozens of *Kanal* trees. If anything was going to be found among the dense overgrowth, more sophisticated gear would be needed. Nevertheless, we looked for the remainder of the day and spent the night at Barre. Going ashore the next morning, we talked to a number of people. The natives knew of the crash landing, insisting the aircraft had come down near Barre. Some told us they saw the aircraft shot down in the distance, but there was no way to prove they had not confused this with something they had seen during World War II. Still more hearsay, though we were closer than we had been before.

That night we returned to Mili Mili and the next day pushed off for Majuro after a final friendly visit with Arik and his family, my hosts on Barre. They had done everything possible to make our visit pleasant, characteristic of the Marshallese (though we had encountered some resistance from Clement and Jororo). Several people had actually seen an airplane with a woman pilot go down. Somewhere there had to be a Japanese eyewitness who could fill in the gaps. I determined that I would devote myself to finding such a person and then go to Japan for official records to back up the story.

Once back on Majuro, I was told of Judge Kabua Kabua, another descendant of Kabua the Great. The judge had been chief magistrate on Jaluit in 1937. He was willing to answer what questions I might have, so I paid him a visit. When asked if he had ever seen or heard anything about the lady pilot, he answered, "Yes, I heard a story about her from the Japanese. Part of the story, I heard . . . her plane ran out of gas and she came down near Mili. The Japanese picked her up in a fishing boat and took her to Saipan, the Japanese headquarters."

Though his recollections were still second-hand, the details were very similar to what I had been hearing. I was sure that I was on the right track. With persistence and time, confirmation of the story was bound to surface.

He also recalled the military buildup in the 1930s, and the four hubs of activity in the Marshalls—Mili, Maloelap, Wotje and Kwajalein. He had worked for the Japanese government for twelve years after graduation from a Japanese school.

With our funds almost exhausted after the trip to Mili, we once again headed for home, this time via Guam and Saipan. My motive was to get some first-hand knowledge of the Saipanese eyewitness accounts and, if possible, talk to a few of the natives myself. Out of the jumble of theories before the public, a common denominator was a white woman on Saipan. If I could get some confirmation of that story, then I would have to consider linking a ditching in the Marshalls with imprisonment on Saipan.

Shortly after our arrival on Saipan we met Florence Kirby and Olympio Borja, who had been told by a farmer that he saw two Americans, a man and a woman, near Garapan Cemetery. Though the farmer was no longer alive, the two women related the story:

One evening he went to the back of his pasture where his cow was tethered. Just as he was approaching the cow, he saw the Japanese marching a man and a woman toward the cemetery. The prisoners were wearing khaki uniforms and had their hands tied behind them and bags over their heads. One was taller than the other, and the skin on their arms was white. The farmer hid immediately and stayed out of sight until almost midnight, fearing he would be killed if the Japanese found him. He believed the two people were executed.

Olympio and Florence also told us of their grandfather, who was imprisoned in Garapan for three months after being caught drunk one night. Though the men and women were separated into different sections, the old man's cell was not too far from the one that was said to be occupied by the American woman pilot. When he caught pneumonia he was released to die, but lived many more years to tell the story to his relatives. The girls' parents owned land adjoining Garapan, and their mother still woke up in the middle of the night thinking she heard screams and moans from the prison. The memories were so painful that she refused to go near the scene of so much suffering.

Florence took us to the infamous Japanese prison at Garapan, now derelict, covered by dense jungle, with thousands of snails crawling throughout and even with trees growing in the cells. Most of the stories dealing with Earhart on Saipan had mentioned this prison, where both she and Noonan were supposed to have been held. When tourists visit the island, they are taken here to see AE's cell. Still remaining in the walls were the round metal rings used to tie prisoners' thumbs overhead while they were seated on the cement floor.

Olympio and Florence told of another incident involving a Japanese policeman before the war. He had been having dinner with his thirteen-year-old daughter when he was interrupted by a number of drunk Japanese police officers. They proudly boasted of killing two Americans, a man and a woman. This upset the policeman, who told them their act was wrong and kicked them out of the house. He told his daughter never to say a word about the visit. She kept the secret until her father died, and then began to tell the story.

All of this was certainly fascinating—but it was still hearsay testimony. If people did not surface who could tell me directly that they had seen the Electra or its crew, then I had the same problem as every other theorist—no hard proof.

After returning to Florida, I let the experiences of the past month sink in. We were very close, yet so far from finding out how AE could have flown such a long way off course. Though Jororo Alibar, the maimed fisherman from Mili, did not wish to talk with me in detail, he had seen a twin-engine aircraft go down near Barre Island, one of many making up Mili Atoll. And he had told Ralph Middle that he saw a white woman and man paddle ashore and bury a metal container. If those two were actually Amelia and Fred, what had been their actual route of flight?

My trips to the Marshalls had been making much local and some national news in the United States, though much of what was reported did not bear any resemblance to what had taken place. The accurate interviews were published under Mark Hanebutt's byline in the Orlando *Sentinel Star*.

Though I was contacted by many people offering help, one man in particular not only became a good friend, but provided research that turned out to be pivotal. Paul Rafford, Jr., had been a communications and astronaut recovery expert with the U.S. space program during the 1960s and 1970s. Even more fascinating, he had been a radio operator for Pan Am from before World War II, and he knew a number of people who had worked with Fred Noonan. Rafford became intrigued with the loss of Earhart in the mid-1960s, when many stories and books were being published. However, his major interest was in finding out how such a famous pilot and an expert navigator could get lost.

While serving on Pan Am's transocean Clippers in 1940, Rafford had flown under conditions very similar to Earhart's and was familiar with her radio equipment. However, Clipper crews used radiotelegraph in those days, while Amelia depended exclusively on radiotelephone. Although radiotelephone, or voice communication, was adequate for short routes within the United States, in 1937 over-ocean aeronautical radio communication and direction-finding required a radiotelegraph operator. In fact, during the layover in Miami just before the world flight began, Amelia's husband was warned by Pan Am officials that her radio communication capabilities were entirely inadequate for long ocean flights.

Rafford wondered what would result if space-age computer techniques were applied to the old *Itasca* radio and navigation logs. Could he reconstruct that last flight and find out what went wrong? I was absolutely delighted not only with his down-to-earth approach but with his potential to explain how the Electra could have gotten so far off course.

From what Paul had heard from his Pan Am friends, Fred Noonan was no ordinary navigator. When he joined Earhart, the news media correctly touted him as a pathfinder on the China Clipper, the famous flying boat that pioneered Pacific airline routes in the mid-1930s. No publicity, however, was given to his firing by Pan Am before Earhart hired him. Paul was told by his friends at the airline that after the Electra's disappearance, whispers spread among Fred's former colleagues that he had returned to the habit that cost him his job on the Clippers.

Paul started contacting other Earhart researchers and found that some wondered why Noonan's celestial navigation had gone wrong during the leg from Lae to Howland. As a Clipper radio operator of the same era, Rafford wanted to discover how Earhart's radio navigation failed her. Even with the crude radio equipment carried on the Electra, Earhart should have been able to get a directional steer to the *Itasca*. With a minimum of effort the *Itasca*'s radio operators could have guided her in. Why hadn't a man of Noonan's ability been able to use the radios to get the Electra to Howland? Rafford assumed, incorrectly as he later learned, that Noonan was proficient in radio operation.

Paul's specialty while manager of NASA's recovery team was the analysis and prediction of radio communication with the ships and planes assigned to locate and pick up returning astronauts. To become familiar with the flight, Rafford studied the direct route plotted for Amelia from Lae, New Guinea, to Howland Island before the world flight. Howland, a tiny speck almost on the equator just east of the international date line, would have taken some excellent navigating and flying to find. Rafford wondered if Earhart actually flew direct, considering that Noonan was said to have been helped aboard the Electra nearly incapacitated by alcohol. Some time during those two days at Lae, had she changed her mind and altered the flight plan?

Rafford traveled to Washington, D.C., where he reviewed the files of the Navy's archives and the Smithsonian Institution's National Air and Space Museum (NASM). There he learned of Dr. Francis X. Holbrook, a dedicated historian who had turned up many new pieces of the Earhart puzzle during the late 1960s. Holbrook had copies of the radio message traffic between Pacific stations preparing for Earhart's departure. In addition, he had corresponded with several people who had heard Earhart's transmissions on her way out of Lae. Holbrook was willing to share his material.

The official report of Jim Collopy, district superintendent of civil aviation in New Guinea, surfaced for the first time in Holbrook's research. Jim had been an eyewitness to Amelia's takeoff, and his account gave the first authoritative statement of the amount of fuel her plane carried. It proved she should have had several hours' worth left when the *Itasca*'s radiomen last heard her voice, even though she thought she was running low.

Dr. Holbrook had also been able to locate and correspond with Harry Balfour, the Guinea Airways radio operator who flight-checked the Electra's radios the day before departure and who talked with AE during the first eight hours of the flight. Finally, through Holbrook's efforts, T. H. Cude, director of police on Nauru Island (between Lae and Howland) in 1937, described how he had heard Earhart's calls as she approached the island, declaring she had its lights in sight.

As Rafford went over these findings, a fascinating fact emerged, hidden from the world for nearly half a century. AE had not followed a direct route from Lae to Howland as orginally planned. Neither had she followed any surreptitious spy route as rumored through the years. Instead, with the help of Balfour, she had made a decision at Lae to fly by way of Nauru Island.

This was news of major importance. It was the first clue that the last leg of the flight had not gone as intended. If this could be substantiated through documentation as well as the recollections

of those who were involved in 1937, then we were on the way toward tracing the Electra's true flight path.

In the spring of 1983 Rafford made another visit to the NASM
library to review its files. The chief of reference services, Phil
Edwards, told Rafford that he could in no way consider his personal search for Amelia Earhart to be complete until he had examined every inch of the Smithsonian's microfilm records on her.
Edwards signed out a complete set of reels to him.

As Rafford later described it, "I walked out of the museum in a
daze, awed by the importance of what I was carrying and ap-
palled by the prospect of spending hours before a microfilm
viewer, particularly when I didn't even know where I was going
to find one back home. But Phil's insistence paid off. I converted
an old camera into a reader—then, one night, there it was, sand-
wiched between some clippings about her disappearance . . . the
actual message radioed to Amelia at Lae from Nauru."

NEW NAURU FIXED LIGHT FIVE THOUSAND
CANDLEPOWER 560 FT ABOVE SEA LEVEL
VISIBLE FROM SHIPS TO NAKED EYE AT
34 MILES STOP ALSO THERE WILL BE
BRIGHT LIGHTING ALL NIGHT ON ISLAND
FROM PHOSPHATE WORKINGS STOP
PLEASE ADVISE TIME DEPARTURE AND
ANY INFORMATION RE RADIO
TRANSMISSION WITH TIMES.

Paul had the confirmation he was looking for. Combing through
Harry Balfour's correspondence with Holbrook and piecing together documentation with other interviews, Rafford slowly
traced the Electra's last flight.

Realizing that Noonan was in no shape to give consistent help
with navigation owing to his severe problem with alcohol, Balfour helped Amelia resolve some of the problems she would face.
He came up with a small departure "window" about two hours
wide the morning of July 2. If Amelia took off before it, she
would arrive at Howland before sunrise; after it, she would arrive
over the initial visual navigation fix Harry had chosen, the Nukumanu Islands, after sunset. The Nukumanus, 750 miles east of

Lae, were critical—they were the only visible aids to serve as a turning point for Nauru and its giant phosphate-mining lights. During daylight Amelia could navigate by using island sightings. Then, after reaching the Nukumanu Islands just before sunset, she could turn toward Nauru with a good expectation of sighting it in the dark within a few hours. After leaving Nauru she would have no checkpoints to guide her before reaching Howland, but at sunrise she could get a north-northwest/south-southeast line of position by having Fred shoot the sun or, if he was incapacitated, from his *Nautical Almanac*. This would give her an approximate indication of how far out from Howland she was, but not necessarily whether she was on course. The middle of the "window" was 10:00 A.M. local time, or 0000 Greenwich Civil Time.

Using the semi-official procedure of sending a radio "note," Balfour relayed word to Nauru Island asking for information about the phosphate lights and the weather. These exchanges of information between radio stations, usually concerning in-house communications information such as operating frequencies and time schedules, were faster than the usual methods. Normally a formal message file was required by law, a system demanding transmissions be passed through each station on the radio net. Depending upon the number of stations and the whims of the operators, this could require a fair amount of time. Amelia needed the information immediately.

Using the net control station at Rabaul to relay their answer, Nauru replied in haste that the lights would be visible all night from as far as 34 miles.

Amelia tried to convince Balfour to go in Noonan's place, because he knew how to use the radios and he had lived in the Pacific most of his life. Harry considered it and later admitted that what really kept him from going was a feeling of impending doom. He also wondered, had he gone, would the Electra have made it to Howland?

As the world knew afterward, Amelia radioed hourly position reports to Harry for eight hours—yet no one but Harry and Amelia knew what positions were involved. Six hours and twenty minutes after she took off, Amelia arrived at her Nukumanu Islands turning point. Later it was plotted by the Navy and re-

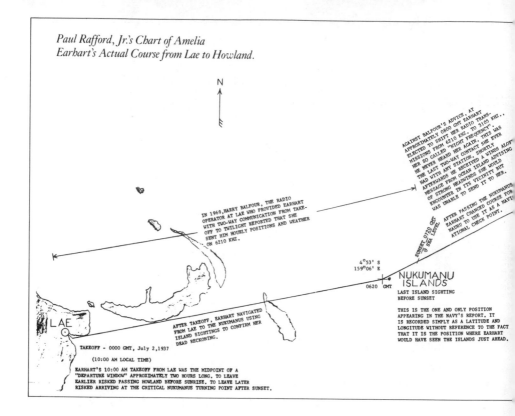

Paul Rafford, Jr.'s Chart of Amelia
Earhart's Actual Course from Lae to Howland.

N

AGAINST BALFOUR'S ADVICE, AT APPROXIMATELY 0800 GMT EARHART ELECTED TO SHIFT HER RADIO TRANSMISSIONS FROM 6210 KHZ., TO 3105 KHZ., HE SO CALLED "NIGHT FREQUENCY". HE NEVER HEARD HER AGAIN. THIS WAS THE LAST TWO-WAY CONTACT SHE EVER HAD WITH ANY STATION. SHORTLY AFTERWARDS HE RECEIVED A WINDS ALOFT MESSAGE FROM OCEAN ISLAND ADVISING OF STRONG HEADWINDS SHE WOULD ENCOUNTER IN ITS VICINITY BUT WAS UNABLE TO SEND IT TO HER.

IN 1969, HARRY BALFOUR, THE RADIO OPERATOR AT LAE WHO PROVIDED EARHART WITH TWO-WAY COMMUNICATION FROM TAKE-OFF TO TWILIGHT REPORTED THAT SHE SENT HIM HOURLY POSITIONS AND WEATHER ON 6210 KHZ.

AFTER PASSING THE NUKUMANUS EARHART CHANGED COURSE FOR NAURU TO USE IT AS A NAVIGATIONAL CHECK POINT.

SUNSET 0720 GMT @ SEA LEVEL

4°53' S
159°06' E

0620 GMT

NUKUMANU
ISLANDS
LAST ISLAND SIGHTING
BEFORE SUNSET

THIS IS THE ONE AND ONLY POSITION APPEARING IN THE NAVY'S REPORT. IT IS RECORDED SIMPLY AS A LATITUDE AND LONGITUDE WITHOUT REFERENCE TO THE FACT THAT IT IS THE POSITION WHERE EARHART WOULD HAVE SEEN THE ISLANDS JUST AHEAD.

LAE

AFTER TAKEOFF, EARHART NAVIGATED FROM LAE TO THE NUKUMANUS USING ISLAND SIGHTINGS TO CONFIRM HER DEAD RECKONING.

TAKEOFF - 0000 GMT, July 2, 1937

(10:00 AM LOCAL TIME)

EARHART'S 10:00 AM TAKEOFF FROM LAE WAS THE MIDPOINT OF A "DEPARTURE WINDOW" APPROXIMATELY TWO HOURS LONG. TO LEAVE EARLIER RISKED PASSING HOWLAND BEFORE SUNRISE. TO LEAVE LATER RISKED ARRIVING AT THE CRITICAL NUKUMANUS TURNING POINT AFTER SUNSET.

corded at 4 degrees, 53 minutes south and 159 degrees, 6 minutes east—the only position noted in the Navy's postdisappearance report.

After passing the islands, she set course for Nauru Island, 600 miles to the northeast. Shortly after sunset, an hour later, Harry Balfour talked with Amelia for the last time.

Rupert C. Garsia, the administrator of Nauru, and most of the island's inhabitants were waiting expectantly for the Electra to pass overhead. As Balfour and Harold Barnes, radio operator at Nauru, had agreed the day before by radio, the mining lights were on to guide AE in. Garsia's wife noted in her diary, "1937. July 2nd: Mrs. Putnam essayed her flight from New Guinea (Lei) [*sic*] and Howland Island. We had notified her of weather, light etc. We picked up her wireless at 6 p.m. but though increasingly loud, we could not make out the speech. She was due near or over Nauru at 9.40 p.m. but though we watched, she did not come near."

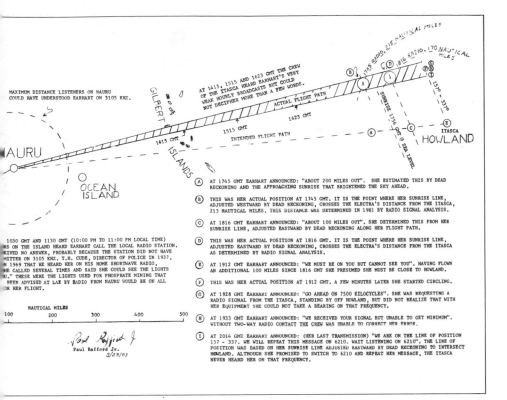

Unfortunately, Mrs. Garsia and her friends were too early. Within an hour the Electra was homing in on what must have been a beautiful sight in the middle of a pitch-black night. Director of police T. H. Cude had the mining lights turned up all the way and listened in on his own home shortwave receiver, a "12 valve, all wave Atwater Kent." He could hear her calling Barnes "between 10 and 11 pm" as she "approached and passed the island" and distinctly remembered hearing her say, "Lights in sight ahead." For Cude to have heard Amelia as clearly as he did at that time of night on 3105 kilocycles, she must have been within sight of the island.

The Coast Guard ship *Ontario* sat in the ocean well south of Nauru, unaware of the new route, waiting for her to pass overhead. It never heard from her.

Finding Nauru, Amelia was as close as possible to beating the odds against locating Howland without celestial or radio navigation. Daylight and a beacon of light had gotten her a little more than halfway. But there were more than 1100 miles yet to cover to her twenty-foot-high destination.

In the darkness the Gilbert Islands, between Nauru and Howland, could not serve as checkpoints. Though the British had radio transmitters on the islands at Beru and Tarawa, they were never asked to assist in guiding the Electra through. Had plans been made to home in on the powerful British radios, it might have been another story. Regardless, Amelia knew the Gilberts were beneath her route and should she miss Howland, she could turn back and land there if enough fuel remained.

Through the night Amelia made hourly radio calls on 3105 kilocycles. At 1418 GCT (1:48 A.M. Howland time) the radiomen aboard the *Itasca* heard Amelia for the first time, beginning a drama of frustration and desperation that the world has come to know very well.

In spite of numerous attempts to get a direction-finding bearing on the Electra, the *Itasca*'s radio operators realized they were trying to guide a crew safely toward Howland that had not even a basic knowledge of radio. When Amelia radioed to the *Itasca* a request that the ship transmit on 7500 kilocycles so she could home in on it, it was obvious she had no idea the frequency could not be used for direction-finding with her equipment. In addition, the DF equipment at Howland was virtually useless on 3105, and if they were to get a bearing she would have to transmit for at least two minutes.

The confusion in the cockpit was as simple as a modern-day radio listener trying to tune in an AM radio station by using a number on the FM band. While the radio operators agonized over why she requested 7500 kilocycles, the channel Amelia most likely wanted was 400 kilocycles, or 750.0 meters, a standard direction-finding frequency. With only a minimal knowledge of radio, it would not have been hard to get the two mixed up.

Without reliable radio direction-finding, the only means left to reach Howland would be a sun line of position found just as the sun broke the horizon at 1756 GCT, as listed in Noonan's almanac. At 2114 GCT Amelia reported this sun line—"We are on the line of position 157-337. . . . We are running north and south."

Confirming this sun line with a copy of the July 2, 1937, *Nautical Almanac*, the same one that would have been aboard the

Electra, Paul Rafford plotted it just as Fred would have during those last hours to find out how far the Electra was from Howland.

Amelia, according to her transmissions, had flown the line and was trying to locate Howland. However, a single line of position does not establish a geographic point. An intersecting line was needed. Flying a line of position was like driving an interstate highway without knowing which exit to take for the destination. If Earhart had been anywhere within 30 miles, she would have seen clouds of black smoke coming from the *Itasca*'s boilers.

Rafford set about determining the exact radio transmitting characteristics of Earhart's Electra by building a nine-to-one scale radio wavelength transmitting model from Smithsonian records. Frequencies, power, antennas—everything had to be exactly like the original if tests were to be accurate. In essence, Paul built an electronic wind tunnel.

Many hours were spent evaluating the *Itasca* radio log entries, translating them into mathematical figures for computer analysis. Could Paul come up with definite figures that would tell how far away Amelia was when she missed the island?

After operating the model countless times, learning the exact radio transmission strength characteristics of the Electra, he fed the findings to the computer program of the *Itasca*'s logs. In test after test the data fell into place with gratifying regularity. Paul's computer estimates of Earhart's distances from the *Itasca* each time she transmitted were intersected with her sun line, advanced east or west from sunrise as required to match her transmitting times. The margin for error in determining AE's position came down to less than 25 miles.

When Amelia radioed, "We must be on you but cannot see you," she was actually about 150 miles north-northwest of Howland, hopelessly off course. Many have said that since her transmissions were so strong, she must have been very close to Howland. Using his model, Paul determined the Western Electric radio would have come in full strength even though the aircraft was so far away.

Unable to find Howland, Amelia had no choice but to follow her contingency plans. As she had told her friends Eugene Vidal and William Miller before the flight, "If we don't pick up How-

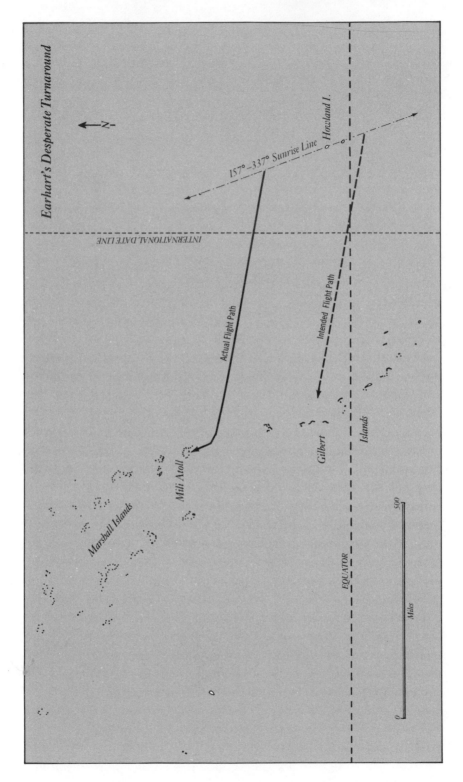

Earhart's Desperate Turnaround

land, I'll try to fly back into the Gilberts and find a nice stretch of beach. If I have to do that, let's hope I choose an island that has fresh water." Presuming their position must have been near Howland, Amelia and Fred plotted a course west for the Gilberts—but since they were far north, they went straight for the Marshall Islands!

Paul had done a masterful job of tracing Earhart's final flight. As he shared his findings with me, I was more determined than ever to get a corroborating first-hand account of her fate from the Japanese themselves in both eyewitness and documentary form.

In February 1981 I was back on the Earhart trail, this time with hopes of getting to Japan. I planned to visit the Marshalls for the fourth time to interview a Japanese medical corpsman who had made the islands his home after the war and to make another trip to Mili—there had to be more information on the ditching the natives saw. If there was enough time I wanted to make another swing through Saipan as well, to trace more eyewitnesses. I still had no idea how Amelia and Fred could have come down in the Marshalls and made it to Saipan, but I was determined to try to find out.

Much to my delight, the Airline of the Marshall Islands had been established a month earlier. I could now buy passage to Mili on a Nomad twin turboprop commuter plane instead of having to duplicate my earlier trip across open water in a small boat. As I stepped off the aircraft at Mili Mili, Queen Bosket and her friends greeted me warmly just as a torrential downpour began. The queen quickly grabbed me by the arm and hauled me into her hut, shooing everyone else outside into the rain, so she could hold court with me as her guest.

After we exchanged greetings and hugs, the rain stopped. I strolled a bit of the island with her and then asked if we could sit down and take up our conversation about witnesses to the ditching where we had left off last time. No sooner had we started than I was told my aircraft was on its way back four hours early from its round-robin of the atolls. Because of an emergency on one of the other islands, we would have to leave immediately.

At the airstrip, by sheer chance, I met Lijon's grandson, Mejin.

Lijon, the friend of Jororo (whom I had met on my last trip to the atoll), was one of those who had seen Amelia and Fred bury the silver container. Dominic, our interpreter on the last trip, had passed on our questions to Mejin, and he was more than willing to help us.

Much to our frustration, Mejin told us we had searched the wrong island for the container and any remnants of the Electra—they were two islands over. Though he had never been there, he knew the location and would be happy to take us there if we could return in the future. I was disappointed in having to leave early, but had we not been called back when we were, I would have missed Mejin with his valuable clarification.

Upon returning to Majuro, I was introduced to Tomaki Mayazo, a coal stevedore for the Japanese before World War II. Though friendly, he was not anxious to tell his story, as if he was not sure it should be told to strangers. Other islanders had told me I should listen to what he had to say, and I did my best to make him comfortable.

He remembered being summoned in the middle of the night, about 2:30 A.M., several years before the war to load coal on a Japanese ship anchored at Jaluit, the Japanese military and commercial center of the Marshalls in the 1930s. As was normal with ships too large to tie up at the dock, the stevedores had to travel out to the ship on a small coal barge to load the fuel aboard.

The crew of the ship was quite excited. They were on their way to retrieve Americans who had crash-landed in the Marshalls. Tomaki told me that, according to the crew, the ship had arrived in Jaluit seven to ten days after the plane had come down. It left almost immediately after he loaded the coal to pick up the flyers and their aircraft, and returned to Jaluit shortly thereafter. Word circulated among the Marshallese that the captured Americans were then taken to Kwajalein and on to Roi Namor, both major Japanese bases in the Marshalls.

As I listened to Tomaki, I tried not to put more emphasis on his story than was warranted. Unquestionably, it was thrilling to hear—I was getting very close to finding out that the Japanese had sent a ship to retrieve the Americans. I did not doubt what this mild-mannered man was saying, particularly since he was so reluctant to share it. But he had not seen the Americans, for they had not yet been picked up. The tension was almost unbearable. Though I was inching closer, I had yet to find what I was after. I hoped my next interview would turn up a bit more.

Bilimon Amaran was a Japanese-born store owner on Majuro who had been a medical corpsman with the Japanese Navy before and during World War II. He was known as a very religious man who had treated the Marshallese kindly. After the war he had come to love the islands and their people enough to settle in Majuro and make his living. He was also known for having had contact of some kind with the lady pilot and her male companion. Though he had been mentioned to me several times, I had not previously been able to track him down.

Somewhat startled when we approached him, he wanted to know how we had found out about him. He made it quite clear that he had no desire to tell stories for personal gain or exploitation. We convinced him that we only wanted to talk about what he had seen of the American aircraft and its crew for the sake of trying to solve the mystery of their disappearance. Jim Slade, a commentator from radio station WMAL in Washington, D.C., who had accompanied me on the trip for the purpose of recording interviews, set up the session.

What followed turned out to be one of the most thrilling moments of my life. Though Bilimon's English was not the best, his straightforward recollections were a reward well worth waiting for. Despite its length, the interview is reproduced here in its entirety because of its pivotal nature.

Jim started by asking if Bilimon could recall the name of the lady pilot and how he came to see her. The quiet Japanese businessman recalled those events of forty-one years past as best he could.

I cannot really tell you what her name was, but somewhere around in 1937 we were called on one of the Japanese military cargo ships. I was working at the Japanese military hospital at Jaluit [where] our director of health services was a military man. We went together to this ship, and we saw a man, he was wounded, right in front of his head and also his leg. And there was a female with him, she about, well, say five—between five and six feet long. She was wearing some kind of a—what am I going to call that kind of dress—it was kind of short. There I am. I saw it.

It was told by the crew on that ship that they found them somewhere between Gilbert Islands and Mili Island, and we treat the man, I personally did. The wound on the front side of his head was not very serious, but the one around the knee area was kind of a four inches cut, inflamed, slightly bleeding while I was treating him. And I heard from our commanding officer, the director of health services, that these people were found somewhere near about Mili Island, south of Majuro. Also I heard among the Japanese, the officers, they talk about how they found them. At this same time I saw, they told me, their plane. It was on the back side of the ship, still in the canvas slings that got it from the water. One of the . . . I think was right or left wing was broken. I wasn't really remember what wing it was, but one of the wings was broken.

Was it a large airplane?

I wasn't quite remember right now. It wasn't very big for me, compared to the present airliners I have seen around. Was not very big one.

Did either one of them say anything to you? Did you talk to them while you were treating them?

Well, the man say something but I wasn't aware of what he was saying because at the time I know nothing about English, so I speak only Japanese so I can understand what the Japanese say, but I don't know what the man was telling me. He say few words, but I don't understand it.

Was the woman fair, and how long was her hair?

Her hair was not really short, it was somewhere below her ear, and she doesn't . . . look nice, good complexion, and I think she was around, somewhere around between . . . I don't know, maybe I'm mistake, but maybe a little over thirty-eight, something like that.

The lady we're talking about was slender, and her hair was fairly short for the time.

Yes, her hair was light . . . light color, sure. And her hair, that's why I say that, her hair was somewhere around about the level of her ear.

She had a very pleasant smile, though I doubt if she was smiling at that time.

Well, I wasn't allowed to go and talk to her. They were being watched by the guard on the ship, except the man. I was allowed to go in and treat him.

He was a dark-haired man with very long, pointed features?

Yes. Well, I was kind of a little scared, to tell the truth. 'Cause the first time I seen American. I did my best to treat the man, but I was afraid to talk to him and even look at him. He had dark hair and blue eyes. I remember the eyes in particular, as they were a very different color from the eyes of the Marshallese.

Do you know where they were taken after you were finished?

I don't really know, but according to my understanding of the Japanese talking nearby, the ship's going to leave from Jaluit back to Kwajalein and then go to Truk and maybe go to Saipan and Japan if possible. That's all I heard, that she'll go from here to Kwajalein and then try to go to Truk, Saipan and maybe Japan if they can make it.

Did they tell you if the airplane was picked up from an atoll, or from a coral reef, or whether just plucked out of the water?

Looks to me they say, if I'm correctly remember, they pick up from the water. They saw them . . . I don't know, I wasn't really sure about that, but the only thing I know, they say their plane was hooked up on the back side of that ship.

After years of searching, I had heard a native-born Japanese tell a simple story of two Americans, a man and a woman, who had crash-landed in the Marshall Islands before the war and been captured. I was beside myself with elation, as were those with me. When I asked why this story had never been told outside his small circle of friends, Bilimon simply shrugged his shoulders and said no one had asked. He saw very few Americans on a regular basis, and what's more, he did not think the story that unusual. After all, the story of the downed Americans was taken for granted among the islanders. I looked away and shook my head. Now I was firmly onto finding out what had happened. Paul Rafford's calculations and tests had placed the Electra far enough northwest of Howland to have made landfall in the Marshalls, and here was a Japanese corpsman who had seen them—or had seen people closely resembling them. If I was going to prove it, I would have to find out which Japanese ships were involved, and their exact movements.

I later went back to talk to Bilimon several times. He never attempted to relate more than he could recall, even though I was tempted to prompt him as much as I could. When he did not remember something, he simply said so. He mentioned again the man's vivid blue eyes, a color he had never seen before in human eyes.* The woman had been wearing pants, and the Japanese were awed that she was the pilot of the aircraft. The crew of the launch that took Bilimon out to the ship was not allowed to board with him and his superior owing to the secret nature of what was taking place.

Though I was not able to make it to Japan, on my way home I reestablished my contacts in Saipan through a friend, Gary Perrin, a schoolteacher there. He introduced me to sixty-five-year-old Ron Diaz, who remembered seeing "a white woman in the back of a truck with Japanese men with her." Though he did not know how they found her or where she came from, "later I learned from friends she was taken from the water. I was told she was in a Japanese airplane that had crashed in the water." He did not recall seeing a white man with her, but heard she was put in Garapan Prison.

This seemed an unremarkable bit of information except for something that made my ears perk up. The white woman had crashed in the water in a Japanese airplane. So many other theorists had tried so hard to give the Electra enough range to make it all the way to Saipan. If Earhart had been put aboard a Japanese ship, then she might very well have been transferred to a Japanese aircraft for the final leg to Saipan. Though this was a small piece of the puzzle, it was well worth having.

*Over the course of the next few years I attempted to find out the color of Noonan's eyes, but there seemed to be no one alive who could remember. At long last Captain Marius Lodeesen, who had served with Fred at Pan Am, was asked by fellow Pan Am Clipper crewman Paul Rafford what Fred's eyes looked like. His immediate reply: penetrating blue-gray.

The identity of the ship that picked up Amelia, Fred and the Electra was my starting point. If I could find which ships the Japanese had in the Marshalls in the summer of 1937, what their missions were and, if at all possible, their daily movements, then I would have some definite ideas about what was actually taking place. And I would be able to either match or discredit Bilimon's account. If his recollections held up, then I would be close to home base.

In the fall of 1981 yet another run through the National Air and Space Museum files produced a remarkable central intelligence G-2 document on Amelia Earhart, dated August 1949. Far from being uninterested in her loss, the U.S. government had pressed the Japanese for as much information as they could obtain. American intelligence agents were unable to find any Japanese Navy records pertaining to Earhart, but interviews were carried out with Japanese personnel who had supposedly searched for the Electra after it was lost on the way to Howland.

According to the document, the Japanese Navy's 12th Squadron, assigned to the Marshalls in 1937, was instructed by Tokyo, after a request from the U.S. government, to send the *Kamoi*, a seaplane tender, and several large flying boats, using the sea to the south of Jaluit as a central search point. Later the survey ship *Koshu* was ordered into the area. Both ships were listed in Japanese news releases of the day as primary search vessels. The Japanese testified that the *Kamoi* led the rescue effort, but no traces of Earhart were found. The investigation was closed.

By December 1981 I was on my way to Japan at last to interview Jyuichi Hirabayashi, who had served aboard the *Kamoi*, and to locate what records could be found. My arrival was certainly different from August 1945, when I set foot on Japanese soil four days before the official surrender. I had flown one of the first few American aircraft into Atsugi Air Base, carrying communications equipment and military police.

Once settled into a marvelous hotel (nothing like my wooden barracks of 1945), I was interviewed by the *Asahi Shimbun* newspaper about my quest for Amelia Earhart. Other journalists and a television station heard of my efforts, and before long I had a number of allies among these newspeople. One reporter told me that he had tried to interview Japanese veterans who had served during the period of Earhart's loss, but there was a loud silence on the subject. The new generation of Japanese wanted to know the truth, many actively searching out contacts on my behalf.

The next day my Japanese interpreter, Ty Yoneyama, and I started to dig into the history of the *Kamoi* and the *Koshu*. We found a recent book on naval ships by a Japanese civilian publisher, which listed the *Kamoi* docked in Japan by July 10, 1937. Because Earhart had gone down on July 2, we suspected the *Kamoi* could not have taken part in the search as reported to American intelligence in 1949. The *Koshu* was listed as a coal-burning survey ship of over 2000 tons, assigned to the Marshalls in July 1937. My first thought was of Tomaki loading coal aboard the ship he described to me. Had it been the *Koshu*?

Jyuichi Hirabayashi, a veteran who had served aboard the *Kamoi* from early 1936 through July 10, 1937, had responded to the ad we placed in several Japanese newspapers asking for *Kamoi* personnel. After my arrival in Japan, we called him and he came to meet us with the ship's log entries, numerous papers and an extensive collection of photos from his tour. We quickly got down to business.

Hirabayashi confirmed that the *Kamoi*, contrary to the U.S. intelligence report, was nowhere near the Marshalls when the Electra went down. The day Amelia was lost, the ship was docked in Saipan, leaving on July 4 for Ise Bay, Japan, where it docked on July 10. All of this was shown to us from the *Kamoi*'s official records.

Clearly the Japanese had lied to the United States in 1949. What were they trying to hide, and why had they gone to so much trouble to make the *Kamoi* appear as if it were on a search mission?

Hirabayashi then described the two types of seaplanes operated from the ship. Both were craned onto the water and retrieved with canvas slings, a method that was short-lived in favor of lift points on the aircraft. Bilimon Amaran had recalled seeing canvas slings around the silver aircraft on the fantail of the ship he boarded at Jaluit. Though he was more intent on treating the wounded white man with blue eyes, Bilimon had not missed this important detail. The Electra would have been recovered in the same way the Japanese picked up their seaplanes.

The names of the four ships in the Japanese Navy's 12th Squadron were provided by Hirabayashi—*Kinoshima* for mine-laying, *Kamoi* for seaplanes, *Yunagi* and *Asanagi*, which were light cruisers. Not only was the *Kamoi* not involved in the search, but the entire 12th Squadron, which was supposed to be combing the seas south of Jaluit, was actually docked in the home islands. The *Koshu* had not been a part of the squadron.

On July 2, 1937, the *Koshu* was anchored at Ponape, where it received orders to proceed to the Marshall Islands and "search" for Amelia Earhart. By July 9 it was on its way, while the *Kamoi* and the remaining 12th Squadron boats steamed for Japan.

Only the *Koshu*, capable of retrieving small floatplanes, took part in what the Japanese promised was a search, but its log entries revealed no search effort. With a specific mission to perform, it went straight to Jaluit and anchored there on July 13. While loading coal, Tomaki had been told by the ship's crew that the ship had arrived seven to ten days after the aircraft came down. Though July 13 was eleven days after the crash, the time frame was very close. The *Koshu* left for several days, and then returned to Jaluit. At this point Bilimon Amaran would have boarded the vessel to treat Noonan. After Bilimon and his commander left the ship, it sailed for Truk and Saipan on July 19, the date the Japanese government officially gave up its search for Earhart. Hirabayashi remembered the *Kamoi* having two ship's doctors, while the *Koshu* had none. It was quite clear why Bilimon and his superior had been called aboard to treat Noonan.

Though we were uncovering crucial elements of the mystery, evidence of official Japanese interest in AE and her fate still had to be found. Our assistant Tatsu Ehara collected the initial batch of records from government sources. He had come up with the message traffic between Japan, its outposts and its diplomatic offices from July through December 1937. A quick run-through revealed the Japanese were watching Earhart's flight as it made its way across the globe and into the sensitive areas near the mandated islands.

When the Electra was reported missing in the world press, messages between Japanese government agencies began to reflect panic over the consequences. Subordinates were not able to make decisions about what to tell the U.S. government and George Putnam as they sought permission to enter the Marshalls to look for the lost airplane and its crew. Though no one at the time thought the Electra could have made it to the Marshalls, every remote possibility was being explored. Dispatches reflected Japanese orders to keep search efforts away from the islands. There was grave concern about how best to mask the situation, since an entire Japanese Navy task force was supposed to be prowling the seas on America's behalf.

Official government pronouncements were released to the international press. These clearly stated that numerous Japanese ships were involved in the Earhart search. The outside world was given the impression that everything possible was being done to find the lost fliers.

The message traffic we found revealed that as internal Japanese diplomatic confusion increased, Vice Admiral Isoroku Yamamoto, later the mastermind of the Pearl Harbor attack, took the matter in tow and sent his own secret messages to aid Japan's diplomats after continual pressure from the West to be let into the Mandates: it was clearly implied from his statements that under no circumstances would Americans be allowed to search for Earhart.

The interviews, documents, reports, correspondence, research and results of countless hours of tracing leads, with the help of so many people, lay before me. At last I could piece together a picture of what had happened so many years ago. Coming home with the Japanese side of the story was like carrying long-lost treasure. After returning to Florida, I was rewarded even more when I learned that one of the 1979 expedition members had returned to Mili just after I had left on one of my later trips and found the rusted remnants of a tin container, including what was left of a hinge. With the help of Dominic and some others, he searched the two islands near Barre Island using a good metal detector for the metal box Lijon had witnessed Amelia and Fred burying. At the base of a very old *Kanal* tree, buried in the sand, he recovered it. Whatever had been inside had become a solid mass of sand and other materials. Unfortunately, he simply broke the mass up and left it scattered on the sand; we will never know what was in that container, and we can only guess why it was buried. Subsequent analysis of the metal showed it to be low-carbon steel used in manufacturing for such things as tin plate and auto-body parts. How would it have come to rest at the base of a *Kanal* tree under twenty inches of coral sand? I was sure that Fred Noonan's small tin container had been found, just where Lijon saw it buried.

The final challenge was to trace Amelia Earhart and Fred Noonan from that last radio transmission on July 2, 1937, to their ultimate end.

Chapter 6

Lost

1937

A<small>MELIA</small> E<small>ARHART</small> was trapped within the tiny confines of her twin-engine Lockheed. Only Harry Balfour and the inhabitants of Nauru Island knew the Electra had not flown the expected straight-line course to Howland from Lae. Amelia had been her own navigator until Fred was able to help, but they had not found Howland.

"We must be on you but cannot see you. . . . Have been unable to reach you by radio. We are flying at 1000 feet." Below the overcast, AE was actually 150 miles north-northwest of her destination, though both she and those on the *Itasca* thought she was much closer.

"We are circling but cannot see the island. Cannot hear you. Go ahead on 7500 kilocycles with long count either now or on schedule time on half hour." Amelia was showing the strain as her voice rose in pitch. It was as if she was isolated from those trying so hard to help her.

Then the curtain of radio silence parted briefly as the *Itasca*'s radio operators tapped out a frantic series of homing signals on the useless frequency AE had requested. She responded, "We received your signals but unable to get minimum. Please take bearings on us and answer on 3105 kilocycles with voice." Amelia made a long dash for five seconds by holding down her microphone button, but neither DF station could get a steer.

"We are on the line of position 157–337. Will repeat this message on 6210 kilocycles. Wait. Listening on 6210. We are running north and south." That was the last anyone in the free world heard from Amelia Earhart.

Over 20 hours had droned by since takeoff. She should have been right on top of Howland Island. Instead there was nothing but reflected sunlight on the vast Pacific. Why didn't the radio operators aboard the Coast Guard cutter *Itasca* respond? She had been so close—at least that is what their radio signals seemed to indicate to both those in the *Itasca* radio room and Earhart. Now there was only silence.

Bucking a southeasterly wind she was unaware of, Earhart assumed she was south of Howland, when in reality she was north-west. As had happened so many times before, she was flying left of her course without realizing it, and whether it was from habit or unexplained drift, this time it could well be fatal. Now, at 20 hours and 15 minutes into the flight, there was nothing to do but turn around and fly the 400 miles back to the Gilbert Islands.

In plotting a reciprocal course, Fred used Howland as his point of departure. But the island was actually about 150 miles south-southwest of their true position. Without realizing it, the fliers were pointing themselves straight into the Japanese-mandated Marshall Islands. Turning west, the Lockheed picked up a tail-wind of about 15 mph and headed away from Howland.

There must have been a great deal to think about as the two Americans watched the Pacific crawl by mile after mile. From 9000 feet, optimum cruising altitude, so many "islands" had come into view, only to prove to be shadows of the ever-present cumulus clouds. They should have been over the Gilberts two hours ago. And now they had flown for more than four and a half hours with nothing in sight.

Mili Atoll was among the thousand dots of land that covered 400,000 square miles to make up the Marshall Islands, remnants of ancient volcanoes that had long since settled back into the sea. The Japanese had already built an airfield on Mili Mili, the major island of the atoll, as a part of their military expansion in the Marshalls. Since the early 1920s the Japanese had hidden their activities in the islands from prying Western eyes as best they could.

After World War I the newly formed League of Nations had mandated oversight of the previously German-held Marshall Islands to Japan, one of the allied victors, for peaceful purposes. Military fortifications there were strictly prohibited. By 1922 the Japanese Navy was limited to a 5-5-3 ratio of ships compared with the U.S. and Great Britain; in other words, for every five ships built by the two Western powers, Japan could launch three. Japanese military officers contested the treaty, saying it doomed their country to naval inferiority.

Though the United States and Japan had been on the same side during the Great War, postwar tension between the two nations soured their relations. President Woodrow Wilson called for the return to China of all land conquered by the Japanese Empire since the late 1800s. For those in Japan who had championed imperialism, the American demand was a veiled threat. It seemed inevitable to Japan's military leaders that war with the United States would come for supremacy of the western Pacific and Asia.

In 1924 Japanese popular support for the militarists was strengthened when the U.S. Congress passed the Exclusion Act, barring Japanese from immigration to America. The Japanese took this as a slap in the face. The gulf widened as the United States denounced Japanese aggression after the seizure of Manchuria and the invasion of North China. Nippon's resolve only hardened.

In order to conceal the militarization of their Pacific islands, Japan formed the South Seas Trading Company (Nanyo Kohatsu K.K.) in 1922 as a civilian organization. With headquarters in Palau, regional offices were established in Saipan, Yap, Truk, Ponape and Jaluit. Japanese Imperial Navy officers and men were assigned to the company and told to wear civilian clothes when ashore in order to play the part of everyday businessmen.

By 1930 Nobuo Onami, an agricultural adviser to the company, was told confidentially by the organization's president to find a 100,000-*tsubo* (about 80 acres) piece of land on Saipan that could be converted into an airfield. Construction started in 1931, and a simple paved runway was completed the next year, later named Aslito. It was camouflaged and referred to as South Sea Bureau Agricultural Farm #3. Throughout the 1930s maps labeled all airfields built by the company as farms for agricultural use.

From 1921 through 1941 the U.S. Navy made repeated attempts to get "friendly" observers or intelligence agents into the Marshalls without success. The United States was well aware that Japan was up to more than peaceful ocean trade, but had no idea of the degree. Members of the American intelligence community argued among themselves about what the Japanese were trying to hide. Were they afraid their efforts in the islands would appear too weak, thus discrediting their image of military might and ability, or were they genuinely trying to hide a major military buildup?

Japan officially withdrew from the League of Nations in March 1933 with no intention of giving up her mandated territories. Just as she considered Manchuria her lifeline on land, the South Sea islands were her lifeline at sea. Though many American military officers, including air-power prophet General Billy Mitchell in 1924, predicted war with Japan, it was not until the secession from the League that an increasing suspicion arose in the rest of the world that Japan might be militarizing her mandated islands.

There were military officers in Japan who opposed the direction being taken by their peers, enough to attempt a coup on February 26, 1936. Their desire was to restore command of the Army to the emperor and his cabinet. But these Imperial Way idealists failed, and as a result, the small clique of militarists became even bolder, able to promote expansionism without opposition. Manchuria could be used as a base to take over China, then perhaps Southeast Asia.

In 1937 the Japanese Navy switched its construction commission from private builders to the Naval Building Division at Yokosuka because it urgently needed strengthening of naval air power. In January the 12th Squadron, including the seaplane tender *Kamoi* and the minelayer *Kinoshima*, was organized and sent to the South Seas area for maneuvers. Aboard the *Kamoi* was Naoyoshi Itsumi, a naval engineer from Yokosuka ordered to survey the islands for extensive military construction.

On July 7, 1937, just five days after Amelia Earhart was scheduled to arrive at Howland Island, Japanese and Chinese troops exchanged fire at the Marco Polo Bridge southwest of Peking. A truce was attempted, but the encounter escalated into a Japanese counterattack.

Though the Japanese War, Navy and Foreign Ministries

agreed on a policy of "nonexpansion" and "local settlement," the Army General Staff, against the policies of Prince Konoye and his cabinet, sent more troops to China to teach Chiang Kai-shek a lesson, fearing he might retake Manchuria, endangering Japanese-controlled Korea and eventually placing Japan under the heel of Russian and Chinese Communists.

What was to be a brief military action turned into war on July 25. Two days later, Konoye announced a "new order" in East Asia to protect Japanese lives. A quick agreement ending hostilities was to be worked out with Chiang, but the Japanese Army clique failed to appreciate the depth of Chinese anger. By October, President Roosevelt responded with his quarantine speech against Japan. On December 12 the American gunboat *Panay* was sunk by Japanese naval aircraft. Reconciliation was virtually out of the question. On the near horizon loomed a major war in the Pacific.

Amelia and Fred could not have stumbled into the Marshalls at a worse time. As the Electra descended over the small islands that make up Mili Atoll, AE did her best to pick out a stretch of land that would allow her to get the Lockheed down with the least damage. The islands of Alu, Ejowa, Aniri and Tokowa passed by; each dot of land appeared to be nothing but a lush, green tropical carpet floating on top of the sea. There was no room at all to set an airplane down without plowing through thick, almost solid, groves of trees. The only alternative would be to ditch on top of one of the numerous reefs surrounding the islands . . . and that would have to be done without much delay if she did not want to run out of fuel and then have to land dead stick.

AE picked the next volcanic remnant, Barre Island with its long northern reef. Low over the reef she brought the throttles back, reducing power. With such a long stretch of coral, Amelia did not have to worry about setting down exactly. As the Electra's nose came up, speed bled off. Fred was braced in back, behind the numerous now-empty fuel tanks, trying to anticipate the force of impact. Though Earhart had been through her share of crash landings, she had never ditched an airplane before.

At the last moment, AE's right hand darted out to bring the throttles to full idle, pull the mixture levers to idle cut-off and turn both magneto switches off. The Electra settled tail first, hit the water, skipped, then slammed into the water full force, catching the coral reef at the same time. As the Electra dug in, the right wing was torn off outboard of the engine and Fred was thrown forward violently, gashing his head and one knee. The aircraft was resting half in and half out of the water, supported by the reef. Amelia and Fred were alive, but they had no idea where in the Pacific they now rested. Neither was going to waste time contemplating the situation. The top hatch was thrown open as Fred brought forward the yellow rubber life raft and provisions.

Amelia carefully helped Fred over the fuel tanks. He was bleeding from the cuts on his forehead and knee. Finding help, much less a doctor, in the middle of this barren stretch of the Pacific would have been a miracle. AE applied immediate first aid to Fred's wounds with the skill she had learned as a nurse in World War I, but with cuts this deep, infection was inevitable.

AE climbed out of the hatch onto the top of the fuselage, pulled the life-raft lanyard and watched the yellow rubber boat expand. Fred eased out with Amelia's help and steadied himself while she rounded up the remainder of the medical and emergency supplies. Both slid down onto the right wing, placed the raft into the water, boarded and pushed off for shore, some 200 feet away.

Jororo Alibar had seen airplanes before. The Japanese had been in the Marshalls for a long time, as masters after the Germans. Large boats and even flying boats ventured in and out of the lagoon and landing strip on Mili Mili.

Jororo, his fellow fisherman Lijon, Anibar Eini, Dr. John and other Marshallese on the island looked up as the bright silver airplane made a turn for Barre Island. For some reason this one was coming lower and lower. When it appeared it was going to hit the water, Jororo and Lijon started to make their way toward the beach. They watched the airplane crash onto the offshore reef in a great shower of water and settle with its tail down. When "two men" emerged from the machine, they produced a "yellow boat which grew," climbed aboard it and paddled for shore. Jororo and Lijon, only teenagers, were frightened, crouching in the *tiriki*, the dense undergrowth, not quite knowing what to do.

Once the crew was ashore, they dug a hole under a *Kanal* tree

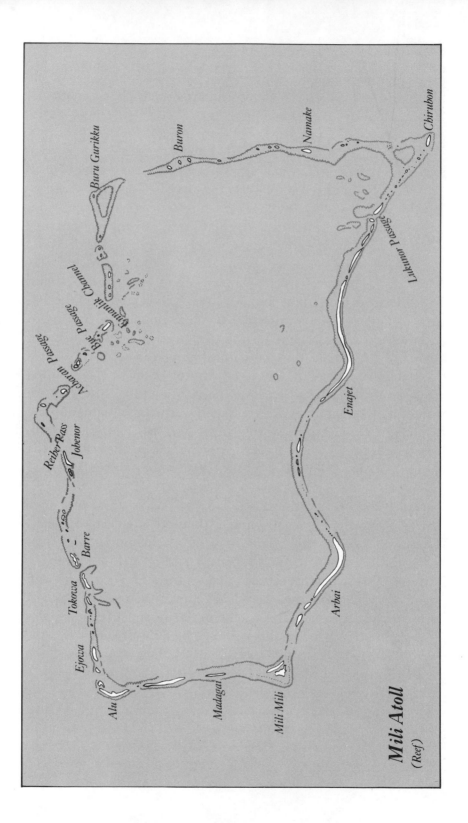

Mili Atoll
(Reef)

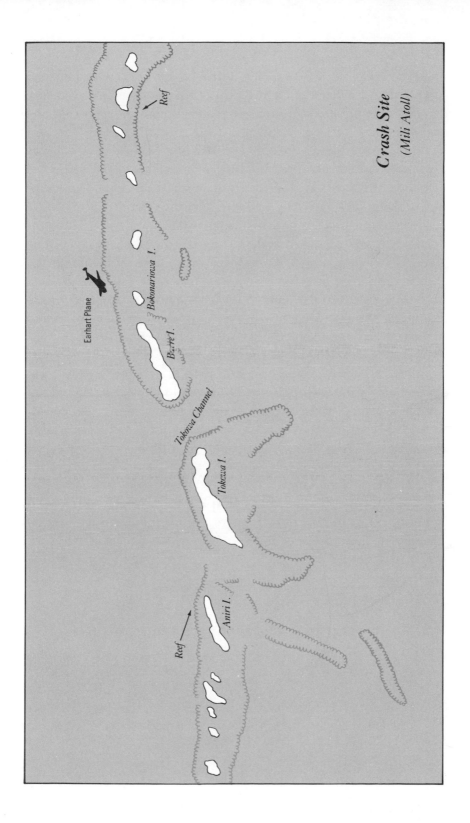

Crash Site
(Mili Atoll)

Reef

Earhart Plane

Bokonariozia I.

Barre I.

Tokorsa Channel

Tokewa I.

Aniri I.

Reef

and buried a "silver" container. The Marshallese were astonished to see that the fliers had white skin (this was their first exposure to that mysterious race) and noticed that one was taller than the other.

The Japanese had heard the approaching Lockheed. As soon as it started to descend over Mili, they manned one of the numerous small fishing boats at Mili Mili and headed across the lagoon toward the spot where they had last seen the aircraft.

Jororo and Lijon watched the Japanese round the island, anchor their boat, wade in and run toward the downed fliers. The two Marshallese now had every reason to be afraid. Life on the islands had been better in many ways since the Japanese arrived, but they were also well known for having little mercy and for demanding absolute cooperation. Neither fisherman had any desire to get mixed up in something that could get them severely punished. They crouched lower into the *tiriki*.

The "two men" made no attempt to run as the Japanese approached. A torrent of animated questions flowed at the white-skinned people. Clearly neither understood a thing. When answers did not come fast enough, one of the Japanese began to slap the shorter of the two white people, who let out a high-pitched scream. This "man" was a woman!

The Marshallese knew if they were discovered they would be hauled off, possibly even killed, simply for seeing the landing and subsequent capture of the strangers. Jororo and Lijon would stay hidden in the same spot until long after the Japanese left with their prisoners. Anibar Eini, watching from another part of the *tiriki*, stayed out of sight as the "lady pilot" and her male companion were put aboard the Japanese fishing boat.

Word of the arrival of the white-skinned fliers quickly went through the small population of Mili. Bosket Diklan, the twenty-seven-year-old Marshallese wife of Takinami, the Japanese commander, knew from the consternation she observed on the faces of the Japanese that these foreign fliers were a problem. Immediately called to Jaluit for questioning, Takinami made it very clear to Bosket that she would tell no one what was taking place. That was something of a joke to the Marshallese, whose gossip had spread the news long before most of the Japanese on the island knew. Nevertheless, the order would be complied with on the surface for fear of punishment.

Amelia and Fred, lost in the Pacific, were now in the hands not of rescuers but of hostile captors. Their elation over being found had turned to fear. Surely the Japanese had reason to be excited, even amazed, at the Lockheed's arrival, but there could not be any reason to suspect that its crew were spies. Their departure from Lae at 10:00 A.M. local time the day before would have put them over Japanese mandated territory in the middle of the night. Amelia and Fred would have been unable to see a thing, much less take photographs. An inspection of the Electra would reveal no intelligence-gathering gear. And besides, Amelia, a sincere pacifist since World War I, would never have undertaken a spy mission in the first place.

Nevertheless, the Japanese had followed Earhart's trip around the world with great interest, for she would be passing south of the Marshalls. The woman flier's route had been logged, with particular attention given to the leg from Lae to Howland. What had the fliers seen as they descended into Mili? The airstrip at Mili Mili was substantial, certainly no farm as the Japanese had claimed. No chances could be taken with what Earhart and Noonan might have seen—they would be held on Mili Mili until a higher authority could decide what to do with them.

The American fliers had dropped right into the laps of the Japanese. Though their presence was secret, the Marshallese on Jaluit got word of the event, and soon the native magistrate there, Kabua Kabua, heard of the capture.

When the Electra did not show up at Howland, Commander Thompson launched a search effort. By 10:15 A.M. local time on July 2, less than two hours after Earhart's last radio transmission, the *Itasca* was under way toward the northwest and the wall of cloud on the horizon. At 2:00 P.M. a general message was sent requesting ships and stations to listen for signals from the plane.

For the next month numerous reports were made of signals that could have come from the Electra, reported to be afloat or on an island. There were even a series of bizarre messages from spirit mediums who had heard from Amelia on the "other side."

The U.S. government ordered an extensive search spearheaded by the Navy, beginning on July 6. The aircraft carrier *Lexington* arrived in the Howland area on July 13, sending aircraft to within 75 miles of the Gilberts and northwest to within 250 miles of the Marshalls. Their only map available showing islands and shoals came from an 1841 whaling book with hopeless inaccuracies. For six days American planes flew 700 feet above the water, each with one-half-mile search responsibility on each side, covering a total of 151,556 square miles. The carrier and three destroyers prowled another 22,640 square miles.

The Japanese were requested to allow American ships and planes to enter the Marshalls, but they sharply refused. They would conduct their own thorough search with the 12th Squadron's four ships, led by the *Kamoi*, and the survey ship *Koshu*.

At 5:00 P.M. on July 6, Lieutenant Yukinao Kozu, the *Koshu*'s radioman, logged the official order to steam from Ponape for the Marshalls and join in the search for Earhart. Through official bulletins the ship's company had been informed of her flight, and they knew she had tried to fly across the Pacific. Thinking the plane might pass by the ship when it was anchored off Greenwich Island in the Carolines on July 2, the crew had been on the alert. The message of the sixth was the first confirmation the Americans were down.

Members of the Japanese Navy Hydrographic Division who had been delivered by the *Koshu* to the weather observation station at Greenwich were asked to search for the Earhart plane in the area. Many such search requests were sent out to various outposts anywhere near the Electra's route of flight, and very few of the recipients knew these requests were not genuine. Yoneji Inoue contacted a native chief, Chu Ai, for help, and made a thorough search in the outer ocean around the island by outrigger. The Navy never radioed back to ask about the outcome of Inoue's search efforts. As a matter of fact, the Japanese in the Pacific who had no need to know what was really happening heard nothing about the search after that. The *Kamoi* and the rest of the 12th

Squadron were at their home port, Ise Bay, Japan, by July 10, when the Japanese told the world this unit was actively searching for the lost Americans.

At 3:57 P.M. on July 9, the small, 2080-ton *Koshu*, under the command of Captain Hanjiro Takagi, sailed from Ponape for Jaluit, where she anchored at 12:12 P.M. on July 13. That night she took on coal. One of those loading the fuel was Tomaki Mayazo, who heard the crew members excitedly mention they were on the way to pick up two American fliers and their aircraft, which had crashed at Mili.

The next day the ship steamed out of Jaluit for Mili Mili, where it picked up both the Electra and its crew. With Noonan in need of more medical attention than could be given at Mili Mili or aboard the *Koshu*, Captain Takagi returned on July 19 to Jaluit, where a Japanese military hospital was located.

The director of health services and medical corpsman Bilimon Amaran were taken out to the ship and allowed to board, while those remaining on the launch were told to stay put until the two medics returned. Amaran was in awe of the man he was to treat: this white-skinned person with striking blue eyes was very different from anyone he had ever seen before. The white woman with him wore trousers like a man and had short hair. The man was cut on the head and had a four-inch gash on one knee. The leg wound was bleeding and inflamed, having festered over two weeks. Amaran carefully cleaned the knee and covered it with a flexible bandage rather than stitch it because of infection. The white man tried to talk with Amaran, but neither could speak the other's language. Amaran was not allowed to speak with the woman.

A silver twin-engine aircraft sat on the fantail of the ship with one wing missing. The canvas slings used to crane it aboard at Mili were still around the plane. From what Amaran and his superior could overhear, the ship was going to sail from Jaluit to Kwajalein, then on to Truk, Saipan and finally Japan if possible.

Tokyo and its various foreign offices had an explosive situation on their hands, facing pressure from both the U.S. government and George Putnam to allow search efforts in the mandated islands.

On the afternoon of July 5 Japanese Ambassador Hiroshi Saito dispatched a coded "Most Urgent" message from Washington, D.C., to Foreign Minister Koki Hirota in Tokyo, relating that the United States had accepted Japan's offer to search for the Earhart plane. By July 7 the situation had become more serious for the Japanese when search orders for the *Lexington* and its aircraft were made public. Consul-General Fukuma in Honolulu reported American plans to Hirota as he understood them from the local English-speaking newspapers, and added, "It has already been five days since the Earhart plane was first reported missing, and the fate of the missing plane is today generally thought to be pessimistic. Despite this, however, the fact that the United States Navy has set up such an exaggerated search plan raises a suspicion that they may be trying to collect materials for strategic study under the pretense of such an air search."

Under no circumstances did Tokyo want the U.S. Navy in the Marshalls. Hirota cabled Fukuma to visit the American naval officer in command of the search effort. Fukuma followed orders, and after meeting with U.S. Navy officials his message to Hirota reflected American assurances that no search patterns would be conducted near Japanese mandated territory.

The situation remained calm until July 13, when Hirota sent a "Most Urgent" message to Ambassador Yoshida in London: "The *Advertiser* here reports that they received a London international news dispatch at 2:00 A.M. today to the effect that a Japanese fishing boat had rescued the Earhart plane. Please verify this and confirm by return." There was panic in the small circle of Japanese officials who knew what had been happening in the Marshalls. Had the truth leaked from one of their classified sources—radio, a letter, a loose statement? Or even worse, had the secret diplomatic code been broken? Would the Americans press them for more details or would they accept this as rumor? A few tension-ridden days passed, and nothing more came of this coincidental near-exposure of the truth. The Japanese officially called off their "search" on July 19, the same day the *Koshu* sailed from Jaluit for Truk. There Earhart and Noonan were transferred to a Navy seaplane, most likely a Type 91 Hiro H4H1, and flown to Saipan, Japanese headquarters in the Pacific.

An eleven-year-old native girl, Josephine Blanco, was on her way to the Japanese military area at Tanapag Harbor at noon on a warm summer day in 1937. With a special pass she was permitted through the gate to bring lunch for her Japanese brother-in-law, J. Y. Matsumoto. Hearing an airplane overhead, she saw a twin-engine aircraft head into the harbor and "belly land." When she got to Matsumoto he told her, "Come see the American woman."

Joining a small group of people, she saw a white woman standing next to a tall man wearing a short-sleeved sport shirt. The woman wore a shirt and trousers. The faces of both Americans were white and drawn, as if they were sick. They were led away by Japanese soldiers. Josephine thought they were to be executed. Though she assumed she had seen an aircraft ditch, in reality the seaplane had simply landed. In later years her statements would be interpreted as an account of the Electra's crash-landing (which would mean that Earhart and Noonan had changed course drastically during their world flight in order to gather intelligence about Japanese fortifications in the Pacific).

Amelia and Fred were taken for questioning to the large three-story hotel that served as an administration building. The Japanese had been fearful that the Electra would fly into their territory; they had followed the flight very carefully and had put their personnel on alert. That the Electra had come down in the Marshall Islands pointed to a spy mission. Earhart was carrying a 35-millimeter camera, incriminating evidence to the Japanese. Though they pleaded innocence, had the Americans seen enough military activity to reveal a violation of international law by Japan? Regardless of the intentions of the woman pilot and her navigator, they could not be released. Things had gone too far. Both were locked up in Garapan Prison.

Two months passed before George Putnam decided to press the Japanese again for permission to search the Marshall Islands himself. His first request, just after the Electra had disappeared, had been curtly dismissed. On September 7 Consul-General Shiozaki in San Francisco cabled Hirota, "Edward E. Brodie, who is a local businessman here and used to be American minister abroad, visited me today and asked for assistance of the Japanese authorities in the search for the wrecked airplane in our mandate islands territory because Earhart's husband, George Plmer [*sic*] Putnam ... who has been eagerly trying to search for the wrecked airplane, thinks that the remains may be found on one of the islands in that territory, 500 miles away from How-land Island. . . . Please let me know how to deal with his request."

Vice Foreign Affairs Minister Kensuke Horiuchi passed the request on to Admiral Isoroku Yamamoto, navy vice minister, who sent a "Strictly Confidential" message back to Horiuchi on September 17: "In regard to the search for the remains of the Earhart plane in our mandate territory, our Imperial nation will have all the vessels and fishing boats in the area make every pos-sible effort to search for the remains." No such effort was made, but the assurances to the contrary would keep Putman and any others out of the Marshalls.

Three months later, on December 3, the Australian magazine *Smith's Weekly* contended that U.S. Navy planes had flown re-connaissance sorties over the Japanese-mandated Marshall and Caroline Islands during the Earhart search and shared the results with the Australian government. Japan was accused of preparing for war against the United States and Australia. Tensions rose for a period and then simmered down.

Six months after the Electra had vanished, official U.S. attention to what had happened to plane and crew waned. The Navy con-cluded that the Lockheed had run out of fuel within 150 miles of Howland. After ditching, it sank and the crew did not survive. The carrier *Lexington,* its planes and its task group had searched vast amounts of ocean in vain.

Amelia and Fred were cut off from the Western world in every sense, and as week after week went by they saw little more than their damp, tiny cells. Japanese imprisonment was hard on both of them. According to Grigorio Camacho, brother-in-law of Jose-phine Blanco and now a retired judge, Fred resisted his captors with increasing intensity. Meals were not usually served at the prison, and the prisoners' families were expected to bring food regularly. As a result, the Americans received very little nourish-ment except a weak soup. Gradually both became ill with dysen-tery.

Resenting the treatment, Fred finally lost his temper and threw a bowl of soup back at his captors. He was taken out and summarily executed.

Earhart, left alone to bear the burden of what must have seemed the impossible result of her last record flight, was regularly taken from her cell for questioning. On the way back and forth from the administration building, owned by the Kobayis, a Japanese family who had settled in the islands, Amelia was seen by several Saipanese. Matilda Fausto Arriola, interviewed by Catholic Father Arnold Bendowske of Saipan,* remembered her family offering AE fresh fruit when she was allowed to stop by. "I thought probably she had some kind of problem with diarrhoea. . . . My mother said, 'That woman looks sickly.' "

The white woman gave Matilda's sister, Consolación, a white-gold ring with a white stone, but it was lost after the war. Matilda also recalled, "Her hair looked brunette to me . . . It wasn't long. It seemed to me like it was a man's hair cut, a little longer, and her face was that of a very strong woman. . . . [This was in] 1937 or '38. . . . It could be July, June probably. . . . My husband . . . said something happened. There was a plane crash and the pilot was a woman. . . . Even the Japanese admitted that this white woman was courageous to do such a thing."

Several Saipanese were offered minimal pay to attend to Amelia's needs, among them Ana Villagomez Benavente. Asked to wash AE's clothing, Ana would see the white woman "upstairs on the veranda [of the hotel/administration building] and I was downstairs and then there were some house orders restricting visitors. The landlords were the ones giving me the clothing to wash, [which] was not Japanese but European. . . . She had . . . not too short . . . wavy hair."

Ana, while visiting her brother at Garapan Prison, saw the woman there as well. "I looked at her several times, but I did not

*Though there are well over two hundred interviews with Saipanese eyewitnesses to the final fate of Earhart and Noonan in Bishop Felix Umberto Flores's files on Guam, many are confusing. Some people saw the two Americans briefly; others saw them over a period of time. Rumors, though often repeated and spread, were discussed, but as rumors and not as fact. Father Bendowske, who conducted the interviews on Flores's behalf, had no reason to doubt the veracity of what his parishioners were telling him. The account here is a summary of those interviews which were the most consistent. Though details often differed, basic facts emerged to form a thread that helped trace the final months in the lives of Amelia Earhart and Fred Noonan.

have a chance to be real close to her because the Japanese were constantly watching me. I was afraid because the Japanese can really give some punishment. . . . She was an American. . . . I saw her at least three times."

Though the Japanese did not voluntarily share much information about the prisoners with the natives, Maria Roberta Dela Cruz was told offhandedly that they were Americans who were in a "plane, having fallen down in the islands south of us in Micronesia. That fact was well concealed." The woman's name also became known. Catholic nun Sister Remedios Castro heard that "the American woman was caught spying. I also heard that her name was Amelia."

By mid-1938, about fourteen months after the crash, Amelia was finally conquered by the disease that had been eating her away inside. The first news that the Saipanese received of her death came with a request for wreaths. Matilda Arriola was approached by a "servant [who] came asking for wreaths. [When] he came back to take the wreaths, I asked him who died. He said the American woman. I said, 'What happened to her?' And he said 'Sekiri,' which is Japanese for dysentery, diarrhoea. It is true that that woman . . . went to the toilet a lot and after that she would go to our house. . . ."

Amelia Earhart and Fred Noonan were the first prisoners of war and casualties in a conflict yet to come. No one in Japan has ever stepped forward with reliable information on what happened from their point of view, but that is not surprising, since the Japanese have yet to admit a violation of international law prior to World War II. The illegal use of the mandated islands for military purposes is strongly denied to this day. Government officials continue to claim the Marshall Islands were occupied for cultural reasons, for fishing and for trade. Even Japan's history textbooks overlook prewar imperialism, demonstrated in such ventures as the South Seas Trading Company's role as a front for the Imperial Navy complete with officers dressed as civilians.

With the capture and death of Amelia Earhart and Fred Noonan, the last great adventure of aviation's Golden Age was over.

Secret Japanese Message Traffic–1937

The following documents shed a great deal of light on the Earhart loss when compared with the logs of the Japanese ships that were supposed to be searching for the Electra. Though the Japanese had announced to the world that its Navy's 12th Squadron was searching the Marshalls along with the survey ship *Koshu*, in fact the entire squadron was in port at Ise Bay, Japan, by July 10, 1937. Yet when George Putnam requested access to the Marshall Islands the following September to search for his wife, a "Strictly Confidential" message was sent out on September 17 by Isoroku Yamamoto, vice minister of the Navy, to all foreign service personnel. In dealing with such requests they were to say that Japan would continue to search for the remains, when in fact no further efforts were made.

1937   13135   Dispatched at Honolulu   July 7 PM
                 Received at Home Office   July 8 PM

To Foreign Minister Hirota
                                    Consul-General Fukuma

#43

Re: Search for the Earhart Plane

1. To summarize the statement made by the commanding officer, Mirphin, which was reported in the evening issue of the local English-language newspaper today, the search plan for the Earhart plane by the United States Navy will be to send out 98 aircraft carried by the *Lexington* to search around the Phoenix Islands, which takes only five

hours. The aircraft carrier *Lexington* is cruising at a speed of 33 knots, and therefore she will arrive in the Lahaina Channel (Maui Island) tomorrow afternoon to load fuel and 10,000 gallons of gasoline for aircraft and will head immediately for the Phoenix Islands. The air search will start on the morning of July 12; until then three aircraft from the battleship *Colorado* will take a leading part in the search around Howland Island, together with the patrol boat *Itasuka* and the destroyer *Swan*.

2. It has already been five days since the Earhart plane was first reported missing, and the fate of the missing plane is today generally thought to be pessimistic. Despite this, however, the fact that the United States Navy has set up such an exaggerated search plan raises a suspicion that they may be trying to collect materials for strategic study under the pretense of such an air search.

大臣　次
電信課ヨリ　1
宣達先　合議　会計　人事　調書　文化　情報　修約　通商　米欧　亜細亜　東亜

第四三號
廣田外務大臣
昭和12　一三一三五　昭
左ノ　ル省
七月八日夜著
傍聞概報事
米

「イヤヘート」機捜索方ニ関シ

一　「マーフィン」長官ノ派遣トシテ本七日英字紙夕刊ノ報道スルヲ後
　ノ概括スルニ「イヤヘート」機捜索海軍側今後ノ
　計畫ハ「レキシントン」搭載ノ飛行機九十八機ヲ以テ「フェ
　ニックス」群島一帯ヲ捜索（俺ニ六時間ヲ要スルノミ）スルニアリ
　「レ」航空母艦ハ三十三涅ノ速力ヲ以テ来航中ニ付八日午後「ハ
　イナ」水道（「マウイ」島）著料及飛行機用「ガソリン」一
　万ガロンヲ積込ミ九日午後出發「フェ」群島ニ向ヒ行スヘク十

二日朝ニハ前記飛行機ニ依ル捜索開始ノ運トナルヘシ夫レ迄ハ戰
艦「コロラド」ノ飛行機三機ヲ中心トシ混洋船「イタスカ」及
驅逐艦「スオン」ヲ以テ「ハウランド」島方面ヲ捜索スヘシ

二　「イ」機ノ消息杳絶エシ以来既ニ五日ヲ経過シ其ノ運命ハ一般ニ悲
観セラレツツアルモ今日米國海軍ニ於テ斯クノ如キ大袈裟ナル捜索計
畫ヲ講スルハ捜索ニ名ヲ藉リ其ノ實軍事上ノ研究ニ資セントスル
モノニアラサルヤ茲ニ一ノ疑問アリ
米ヘ様電セリ

外務省

July 13, 1937   11:20 AM

To Ambassador Yoshida, England

Foreign Minister Hirota

#270 (Most Urgent)

Re: Rescue of the Earhart Plane

The *Advertiser* here reports that they received a London international
news dispatch at 2:00 A.M. today to the effect that a Japanese fishing boat
had rescued the Earhart plane.
Please verify this and confirm by return.

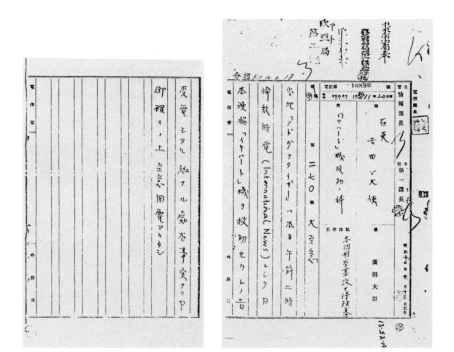

1937   13690   Dispatched at Washington, D.C.   July 13 PM
                 Received at Home Office   July 14 AM

To Foreign Minister Hirota

Ambassador Saito

#252

Re: Ours #233

When I saw the Secretary of State on July 12, he expressed his gratitude for the Japanese cooperation in the search and said that the members of the United States Congress were very pleased about the Japanese goodwill, and at the same time he informally mentioned that the rescue of Earhart was no longer considered to be hopeful.

1937   21796   Dispatched at San Francisco   Sept 7 PM
                Received at Home Office   Sept 8 PM

To Foreign Minister Hirota

Consul-General Shiozaki

#117

Edward E. Brodie, who is a local businessman here and used to be American minister abroad, visited me today and asked for assistance of the Japanese authorities in the search for the wrecked airplane in our mandate islands territory because Earhart's husband, George Plmer [*sic*] Putnam (who is Brodie's judge [?] and a member of the New York publishing Putnam family), who has been eagerly trying to search for the wrecked airplane, thinks that the remains may be found on one of the islands in that territory, 500 miles away from Howland Island, as there is a tide near Howland Island streaming toward the Marshall Islands at 20 miles per hour. He said he will appreciate it if he is informed of the possible cost of the operation, for which he is prepared to pay. Please let me know how to deal with his request. In the meantime, I told him that I would convey his request to the Home Office but that he should also ask the United States government to contact the Japanese government to this effect, which please note.

September 10, 1937

To Vice Minister, Ministry of the Navy
    Vice Minister, Ministry of Colonial Affairs

Vice Minister Horiuchi
Ministry of Foreign Affairs

Re: Search for the Earhart Plane

In regard to Amelia Earhart, who met with disaster near Howland Island in the South Pacific, her husband, George Palmer Putnam, has
since been eagerly trying to search for the wrecked airplane and, in this
connection, Edward E. Brodie, who is a San Francisco businessman and
used to be American minister abroad, visited our San Francisco Consul-
General Shiozaki on September 7 and asked for Japanese assistance in
the search for the wrecked airplane in our mandate islands territory, as
there is a tide near Howland Island streaming toward the Marshall Islands at 20 miles per hour and consequently the remains of the Earhart
plane may be found on one of the islands in that territory, 500 miles
away from Howland Island. He said he would bear the cost of such a
search operation by the Japanese and wanted to know, if possible, about
how much the cost would be. Consul-General Shiozaki told him that the
United States government should also make such a request. It is necessary for the Consul-General to respond to the request; therefore please
let me have your views as soon as possible. Putnam, who is the person
concerned with this search, is a friend of Brodie and a member of the
New York publishing Putnam family, which please note for your reference.

10 138

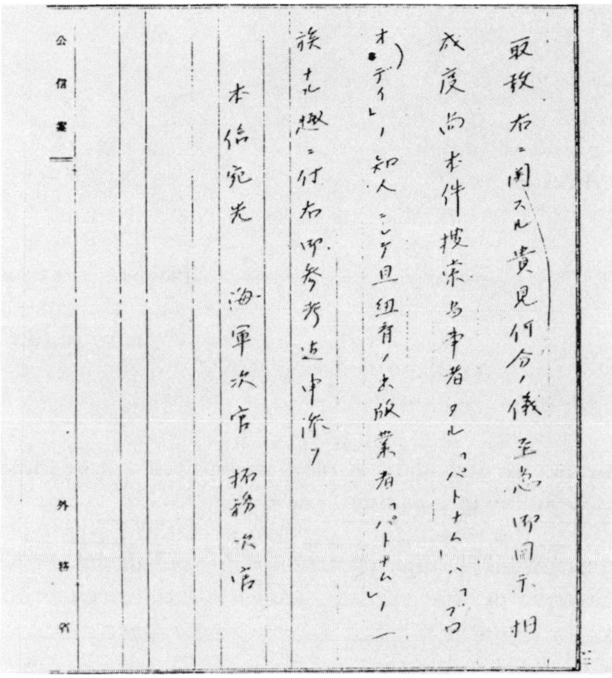

取敢右ニ関スル貴見何分ノ儀至急御回示相
成度尚本件捜索当事者タル「パトナム」ハ「プロ
オ・デイ」ノ知人ニシテ且紐育ノ出版業者「パトナム」ノ一
族ナル趣ニ付右御参考迄申添フ
本信宛先　海軍次官　拓務次官

公信案　外務省

峡ニ漂着シ居ルヤニモ推測セラルル趣ヲ以テ同方
面ニ於ケル捜索ニ関シ日本側ノ援助ヲ得度ク
且右日本側ノ援助捜索ニ要スル費用ハ自ラ
負担スヘキニ付出来得レハ右概略許可ナルヘ
キヤヲ承知シ度キ旨願出タル趣ナリ　本件ニ関シ
右本人ニ対シ塩崎総代ヨリ
入サナシ[illegible]コトナニ旨申入[illegible]
テハ米国政府ヨリモ何等申出[illegible]知レナ
関
本省[illegible]総領事ニ於テ回答ノ都合モアリ　不
[illegible]内ナルモ

公信案　外務省

13-58-B

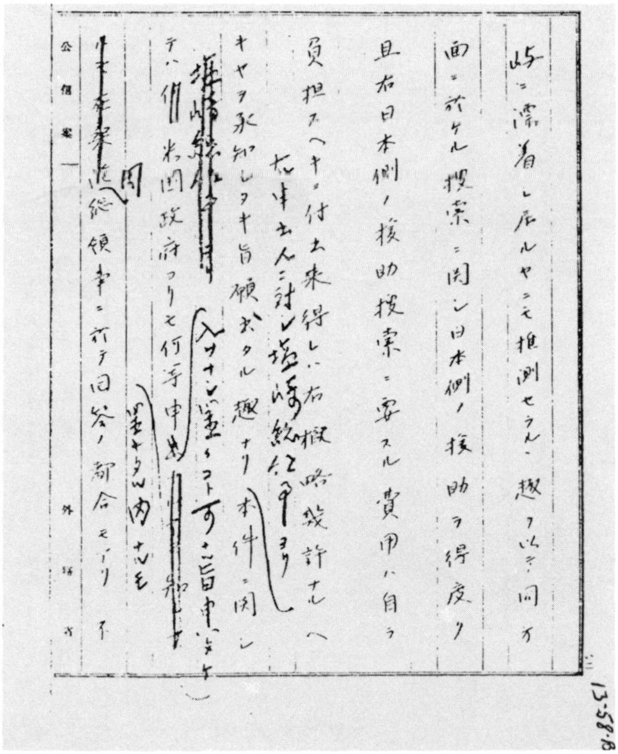

STRICTLY CONFIDENTIAL

September 17, 1937

To Mr. Kensuke Horiuchi
Vice Minister
Ministry of Foreign Affairs

Isoroku Yamamoto
Vice Minister
Ministry of the Navy

Re: Search for the Earhart Plane

With reference to the above-captioned subject, please deal with the matter in the following manner:

In regard to the search for the remains of the Earhart plane in our mandate territory, our Imperial nation will have all the vessels and fishing boats in the area make every possible effort to search for the remains.

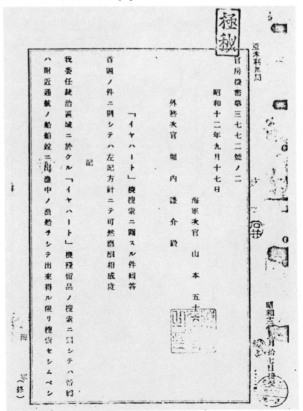

Associated Press #19   December 3, 1937

"Aerial Reconnaissance of the South Sea Islands"
London   AP   December 2

Cavalcade magazine reported a sensational article that, quoting from an article that appeared in the Australian weekly magazine *Smith's Weekly*, the United States Navy planes made aerial reconnaissance of the Japanese South Sea mandate territory when they searched for Amelia Earhart, a woman pilot reported missing in the Pacific. The article reads as follows:

> The United States Navy planes made aerial reconnaissance of some of the Japanese South Sea mandate islands and reported their findings to the Australian Government. In this connection, *Smith's Weekly* reports as follows:
> "With the world situation as it is today, and with Australia's neglect of defence over the years, it was an opportunity not to be missed for Australia to ask the United States Navy to reconnoiter the Japanese South Sea mandate territory. There has been an understanding between America and Australia regarding the matter of this nature."

December 6, 1937   #130

To Consul-General Wakamatau
    Sydney

                    Foreign Minister Hirota

The Associated Press dispatch in London reports as attached. Please try to obtain and send two copies of *Smith's Weekly* carrying an article regarding Madame Earhart reported missing in the Pacific this summer.

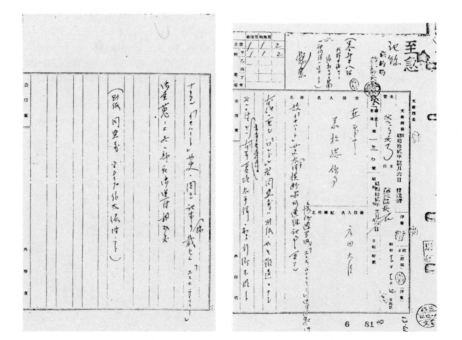

January 14, 1938

To Foreign Minister Hirota

Consul-General Wakamatsu
Sydney

With reference to yours #130 dated December 6, 1937, regarding Madame Earhart, I tried everywhere possible but have been unable to find the original copies of *Smith's Weekly,* and therefore I am sending you two typewritten copies of the entire article.

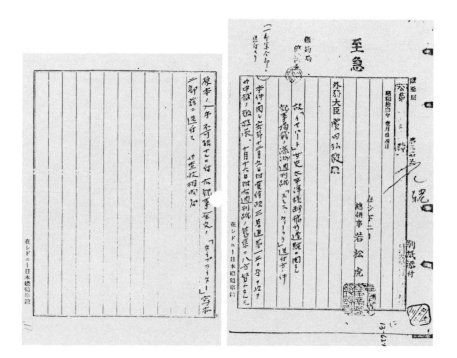

"SMITH'S WEEKLY" - October 16th, 1937.

When W.M. Hughes, at the Peace Conference, insisted that Japan have no island Mandates in the Pacific below the equator, he was long-sighted. But even with what Japan has, her strategists have not been idle. Australian Defence authorities know all about this now. Q.E.D., observers seized the opportunity offered by the search for Amelia Earhart. They swept wide enough to make a scrutiny of Japanese naval activities in the island groups under control of Nippon.

Until now the real story has been withheld of the desperate international intrigue, bracketing Australia, that went with the search for ill-fated Amelia Earhart, when the intrepid aviatrix crashed into the Pacific somewhere near the Phoenix Islands. It is a story of military tactics that went hand in hand with that search — hand in hand with the terrific expense of £500,000 spent on American naval planes.

American planes did more than just search for Amelia Earhart. They cut a wide swathe over the Pacific and circled over the Caroline and the Marshall Islands.

Here Australia comes into the picture. The grim threat of war bears a little closer when it is realised that the groups of islands, and another (Yap) controlled by Japan, lie right at Australia's northern door.

Under cover of the search for the missing aviatrix, America's naval aircraft were anxious to glimpse two of the islands, believed by military experts to have been fortified by the Japanese. The Australian Government now knows more about that search than has been disclosed publicly.

No-one is permitted to land on the Japanese controlled islands. Missionaries who

-2-

previously conducted religious propaganda among natives have been forbidden to return.

The islands are held by mandate given to Japan when that country was a member of the League of Nations. Now she is no longer a member, but she holds the islands in an iron grip. The position of the islands and their possible fortification in the Pacific were matters of grave concern to America and to Australia.

With an examination of the accompanying map it can be seen that this group of islands dominates the Pacific - close to Honolulu, close to the Phillipines, and equally close to New Guinea and Queensland.

When Japan struck so suddenly at China, and its war machine blockaded Shanghai, the doctrine of naked force was revealed. The "I cannot happen nowadays" theory was bayoneted out of existence.

Australia's interest lies in the fact that country, and with the usual lack of publicity, Japan has been working to get closer to the Commonwealth, equipping Japanese bases admirably suited for an expedition into the Pacific.

While this does not allege that Japan is feverishly waiting to strike into the Pacific, military circles are perturbed by the knowledge that fortified islands have been so suddenly prepared nearby.

The knowledge does not add to a feeling of security, when armies march into foreign countries practically without warning these times, and start to "mop up".

As a matter of military precaution plans are always drawn up guarding a mythical invader. In Australia the experts are not the only ones who know of the country's weakness in case of attack. Most people know it, as well as Japan's experts would also know it.

Japan's mandate over the Caroline and the Marshall Islands, plus the taking over (peacefully) of Yap, are matters probably forgotten in the general rush of events. Military and bureau aware of the fact with the seeping through of news that there is a

-3-

prohibition on visitors.

This is grim news to the War Department. It means that there are military occupation, fortification, bases, and war material prying eyes are not permitted to see in cases like these.

So when Amelia Earhart went down and her faint distress signals located her plane around the Phoenix Islands, the search for her gave the pretext that was needed. Sentiment comes second to Secret Service.

Q.E.D. naval planes swept over the waters around Phoenix Islands and then took a side turn and went farther on. They circled on, covering the areas in which the Caroline and Marshall Islands are to be found.

Real flying men are admirable observers. It is their profession.

America poured money on this search. Allowing for the human interest, the search was so costly that only those on the inside even guessed at the purpose of the expenditure of 2,500,000 dollars - in our currency £500,000.

It was the opportunity not to be missed, a real excuse to fly over Japan's islands-by-mandate, to observe what the waters contain. Today the Australian Government has been apprised of some of the knowledge gleaned. With the world situation as it is, and with Australia's neglect of defence over the years, the knowledge came as a godsend - not for by the Q.E.D.

Yap island is close to the equator. If a line were drawn from Japan to the Caroline Islands and then continued to the equator, it would strike Yap. The latter is outside New Guinea, and not so far, after that, from Queensland.

The Marshall Islands are between the Carolines and Honolulu, hence America's interest. From the Carolines to New Guinea is little farther than from Tokio to Shanghai. The map tells the story - and it is a chapter which brings Japan to Australia's back-door.

-4-

Feverish interest in the Earhart search acted, with shrewd newspaper reports, as a blanket over this astounding aspect of the Q.E.D. flights. The facts are known in the proper quarter, which are admittedly perturbed over the Japanese situation in the Pacific.

Even if Japan had no ambitions in the Pacific, other than safeguarding her lines of communications, the proximity of fortified islands would be disturbing enough.

Military men declare that Japanese men and, which come down to demonstrate at times, have Japanese naval men in charge; that they are excellent weapons for scouting and rating thinly settled places, and that the Japanese navigators know the Queensland coast in every detail.

Theoretically, an attack by seamen would be a raid of these vessels loading light tanks and supplies for putting ashore without difficulty. Some of the seaplanes draw only 2 ft. of water, making approach to land an easy matter for the landing of tanks and light supplies.

An Australian who was formerly a high official in the Commonwealth diplomatic services, tells "Smith's Weekly":

"There has been an understanding between America and Australia regarding the Pacific for years. The U.S.A.'s quadrilateral range over the Pacific was a square embracing the area from the Aleutian Islands, Panama, Samoa, and Guam. The Japanese infiltration has pushed the Japanese crescent into the Pacific, forcing American interest back accordingly.

"Japan has a naval base and arsenal at Borrin, and in addition to the mandated Caroline and Marshall Islands (7100 of them) has extended to Guam and Yap.

"Furthermore, Japan's interest in the Phillipines is extensive, with one-third of the population and two-thirds of the trade. The Phillipines will have autonomy in two years, passing out of American direct control.

"Borrin lies opposite the British Singapore base, and now Japan has an interest at Yampi Sound. Take a map, and you will see that a line from Yampi (Australia)

-5-

to Borrin cuts off Singapore, while Japanese infiltration of the Pacific now extends down to Yap.

"You might also like to know that the nearest capital city to Borrin is not in Australia. It is Manila, in the Phillipines, now becoming Japanese in influence.

"I trust", he added, "you know a little more about the Pacific situation. Some of us have known for years, but reports to the Commonwealth Government are probably decorating some handsome pigeonholes.

February 10, 1938

To Captain Nishida
    Navy General Staff

Section Chief of Tzhizu
Ministry of Foreign Affairs

With reference to *Smith's Weekly* carrying an article regarding Madame Earhart, I am sending you a copy of the related article received from Consul-General Wakamatsu at Sydney.

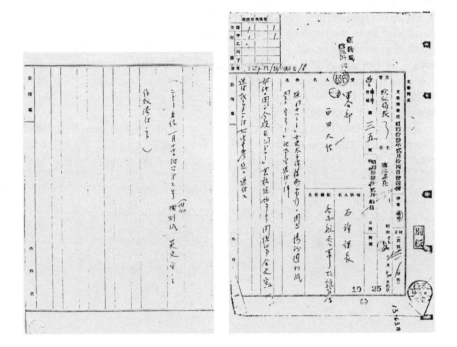

Central Intelligence
G-2 Memorandum–1949

After the war, U.S. intelligence (G-2) was ordered to investigate the Earhart disappearance from the Japanese side. The resulting report, reproduced here for the first time, is remarkable in that the Japanese managed to convince G-2 they had searched the Marshalls quite thoroughly when in fact they had not. The 12th Squadron and the *Kamoi* were listed as having searched the area when, as found in their logs, they were in port in Japan. The *Koshu* was also listed as part of the search, but as having found nothing.

The Japanese lied quite convincingly both in 1937 and in 1949, but their statements could not be proven as such until the ships' movements were determined through research in Japan in 1981.

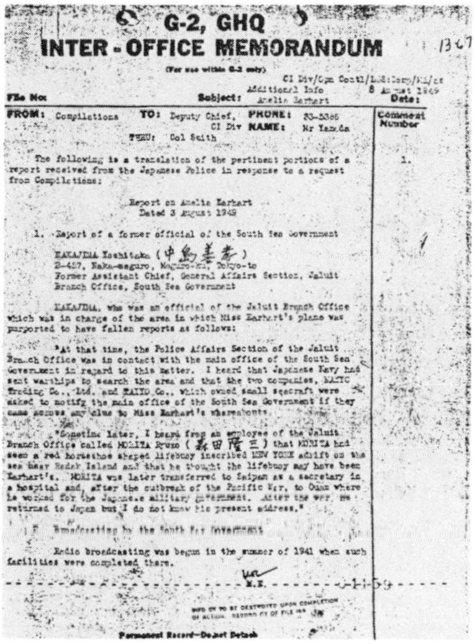

G-2, GHQ

INTER-OFFICE MEMORANDUM

(For use within G-2 only)

1367

File No:

Subject: Additional Info Amelia Earhart

CI Div/Ops Contl/L&S:Comp/KI/cs

Date: 8 August 1949

FROM: Compilations TO: Deputy Chief, CI Div PHONE: 33-5386 NAME: Mr Yamada

THRU: Col Smith

Comment Number: 1.

The following is a translation of the pertinent portions of a report received from the Japanese Police in response to a request from Compilations:

Report on Amelia Earhart
Dated 3 August 1949

1. Report of a former official of the South Sea Government

NAKAJIMA Yoshitaka (中島善孝)
2-437, Naka-meguro, Meguro-ku, Tokyo-to
Former Assistant Chief, General Affairs Section, Jaluit Branch Office, South Sea Government

NAKAJIMA, who was an official of the Jaluit Branch Office which was in charge of the area in which Miss Earhart's plane was purported to have fallen reports as follows:

"At that time, the Police Affairs Section of the Jaluit Branch Office was in contact with the main office of the South Sea Government in regard to this matter. I heard that Japanese Navy had sent warships to search the area and that the two companies, NANYO Trading Co., Ltd. and KAIYO Co., which owned small seacraft were asked to notify the main office of the South Sea Government if they came across any clue to Miss Earhart's whereabouts.

"Sometime later, I heard from an employee of the Jaluit Branch Office called MORITA Ryuzo (森田隆三) that MORITA had seen a red horseshoe shaped lifebuoy inscribed NEW YORK adrift on the sea near Radak Island and that he thought the lifebuoy may have been Earhart's. MORITA was later transferred to Saipan as a secretary in a hospital and, after the outbreak of the Pacific War, to Guam where he worked for the Japanese military government. After the war, he returned to Japan but I do not know his present address."

2. Broadcasting by the South Sea Government

Radio broadcasting was begun in the summer of 1941 when such facilities were completed there.

M.Y.

INFO CY TO BE DESTROYED UPON COMPLETION OF ACTION. RECORD CY OF FILE NR

Permanent Record—Do not Detach

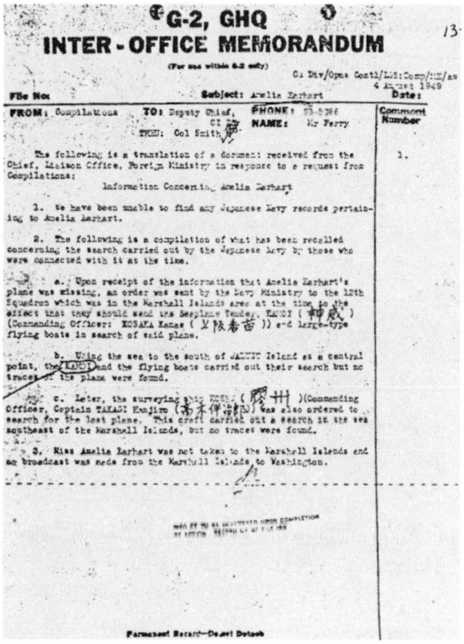

G-2, GHQ

INTER-OFFICE MEMORANDUM

(For use within G-2 only)

13-

File No:

Subject: Amelia Earhart

CI Div/Opns Contl/L&S:Comp/KI/as

Date: 4 August 1949

FROM: Compilations TO: Deputy Chief, CI Div PHONE: 33-5366 NAME: Mr Perry

THRU: Col Smith

Comment Number: 1.

The following is a translation of a document received from the Chief, Liaison Office, Foreign Ministry in response to a request from Compilations:

Information Concerning Amelia Earhart

1. We have been unable to find any Japanese Navy records pertaining to Amelia Earhart.

2. The following is a compilation of what has been recalled concerning the search carried out by the Japanese Navy by those who were connected with it at the time.

a. Upon receipt of the information that Amelia Earhart's plane was missing, an order was sent by the Navy Ministry to the 12th Squadron which was in the Marshall Islands area at the time to the effect that they should send the Seaplane Tender, KAMOI (神威) (Commanding Officer: KOSAKA Kanae (上阪香苗)) and large-type flying boats in search of said plane.

b. Using the sea to the south of JALUIT Island as a central point, the KAMOI and the flying boats carried out their search but no traces of the plane were found.

c. Later, the surveying ship KOSHU (膠州) (Commanding Officer, Captain TAKAGI Hanjiro (高木伴治郎)) was also ordered to search for the lost plane. This craft carried out a search in the sea southeast of the Marshall Islands, but no traces were found.

3. Miss Amelia Earhart was not taken to the Marshall Islands and no broadcast was made from the Marshall Islands to Washington.

INFO CY TO BE DESTROYED UPON COMPLETION OF ACTION. RECORD CY OF FILE NR

Permanent Record—Do not Detach

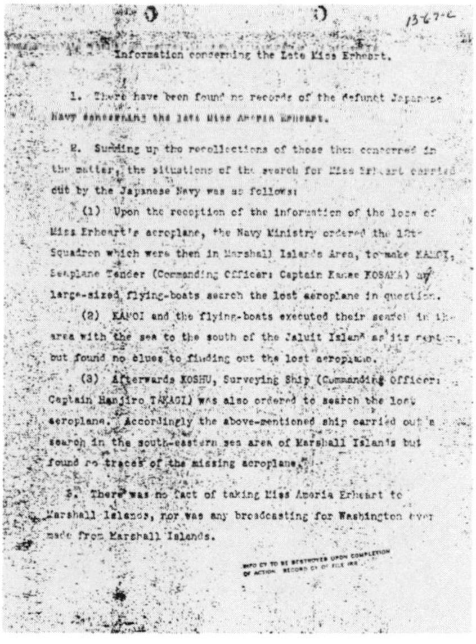

13-67-C

Information concerning the Late Miss Erheart.

1. There have been found no records of the defunct Japanese Navy concerning the late Miss Ameria Erheart.

2. Summing up the recollections of those then concerned in the matter, the situations of the search for Miss Erheart carried out by the Japanese Navy was as follows:

(1) Upon the reception of the information of the loss of Miss Erheart's aeroplane, the Navy Ministry ordered the 12th Squadron which were then in Marshall Island's Area, to make KAMOI, Seaplane Tender (Commanding Officer: Captain Kanae KOSAKA) and large-sized flying-boats search the lost aeroplane in question.

(2) KAMOI and the flying-boats executed their search in the area with the sea to the south of the Jaluit Island as its center, but found no clues to finding out the lost aeroplane.

(3) Afterwards KOSHU, Surveying Ship (Commanding Officer: Captain Hanjiro TAKAGI) was also ordered to search the lost aeroplane. Accordingly the above-mentioned ship carried out a search in the south-eastern sea area of Marshall Islands but found no traces of the missing aeroplane.

3. There was no fact of taking Miss Ameria Erheart to Marshall Islands, nor was any broadcasting for Washington ever made from Marshall Islands.

INFO CY TO BE DESTROYED UPON COMPLETION OF ACTION. RECORD CY OF FILE NR

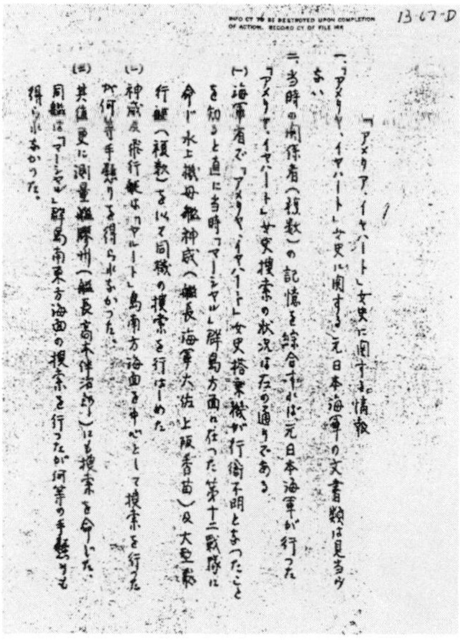

INFO CY TO BE DESTROYED UPON COMPLETION OF ACTION. RECORD CY OF FILE NR

13-67-D

「アメリア、イヤハート」女史に関する情報

一、「アメリヤ、イヤハート」女史に関する元日本海軍の文書類は見当らない

二、当時の関係者（複数）の記憶を綜合すれば元日本海軍が行った「アメリヤ、イヤハート」女史捜索の状況は左の通りである

（一）海軍省で「アメリヤ、イヤハート」女史搭乗機が行衛不明となつたことを知ると直に当時「マーシャル」群島方面に在った第十二戦隊に命じ水上機母艦神威（艦長海軍大佐上阪香苗）及大型飛行艇（複数）を以て同機の捜索を行はしめた

（二）神威及飛行艇は「ヤルート」島南方海面を中心として捜索を行ったが何等手懸りを得られなかった。

（三）其後更に測量艦膠州（艦長高木伴治郎）にも捜索を命じた。同艦は「マーシャル」群島南東方海面の捜索を行ったが何等の手懸りすも得られなかった。

13-67-E

復二ラ二一九一号
昭和二十四年八月二日

外務省　連絡局長殿

引揚援護庁復員局〇〇復員局残勢処理部長

「アミリヤ・イヤハート」女史ニ関スル情報（回答）

昭和二十四年七月二十五日ＣＩＤカラ口頭要求ガアツタ首題ノ件ニ関シ当庁デ調査シ得タトコロハ別紙ノ通リデアル。

尚、当時ノ新聞ニ「アミリヤ・イヤハート」夫人ガ日本漁船ニ救助セラレタトノ説ガ「ロンドン」ニハ流レテヰル（東京朝日七月十五日夕刊）故救助説ハ事実無根ナリト判明シタ（東京朝日七月十四日夕刊）トノ記事ガ有ルカラ申添ヘル

（終）

13-67-F

三、「アミリヤ・イヤハート」女史ヲ「マーシヤル」群島ニ（北ヘ行ツタコトハ無イ）又「マーシヤル」群島方面カラ華府向放送ヲ行ツタコトモ無イ

（終）

INFO CY TO BE DESTROYED UPON COMPLETION
OF ACTUAL RECORD CY OF FILE HM

13-69-

回八三

調　直　書

二、行方不明ノ午前〇〇〇〇〇〇

アメリカノ女流飛行家

昭和十二年七月一日、三十九歳「アミリヤ」ハ出発シテ……イヤハート女史ハ〇〇〇〇〇〇〇〇〇〇十一日午前……桟橋カラ「一千五百哩間ノ燃料ヲ分ケテノ土地ヲ発見ス〇〇上以上十時三十分……「ＳＯＳ」ト打交ス行方不明ト

三、捜索ノ状況……

13-67-H

INFO CY TO BE DESTROYED UPON COMPLETION
OF ACTUAL RECORD CY OF FILE HM

五、又関係方面〇〇〇〇〇〇

「エヤハート女史」ハアメリカ政府ノ〇〇密ノ使命ヲ帯ビ日〇ノ内情ヲ偵察シ自分ハ日本ノ捕虜トナリ逮捕サレル……

ト云フコト〇〇新聞社〇〇……

ト結ンデヰルコト……

昭和十二年七月二日、ガ北緯北豪州〇岸ニ墜落レ

（終）

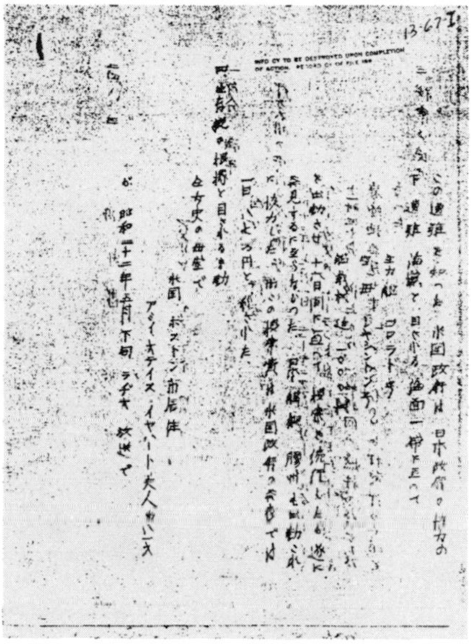

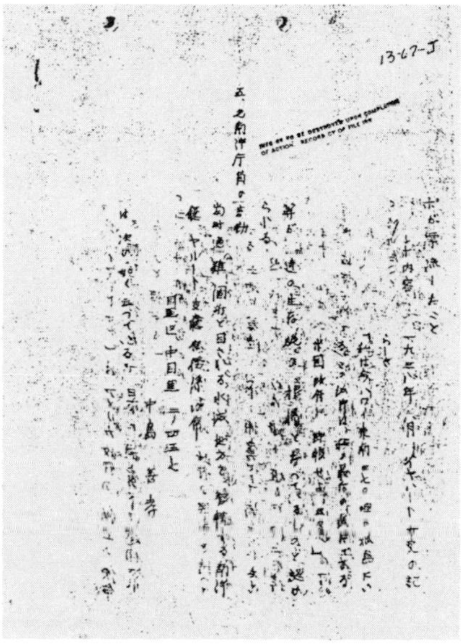

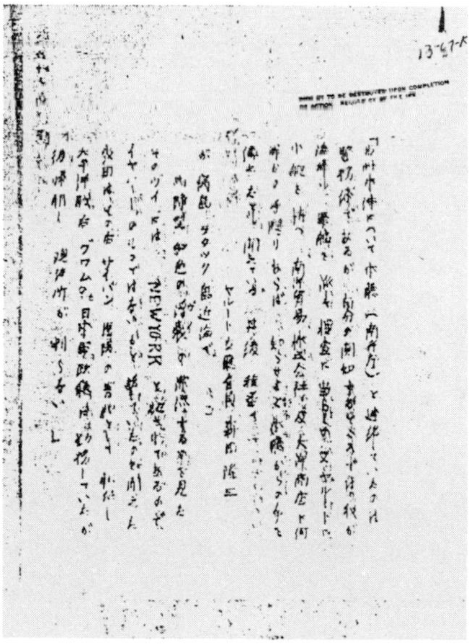

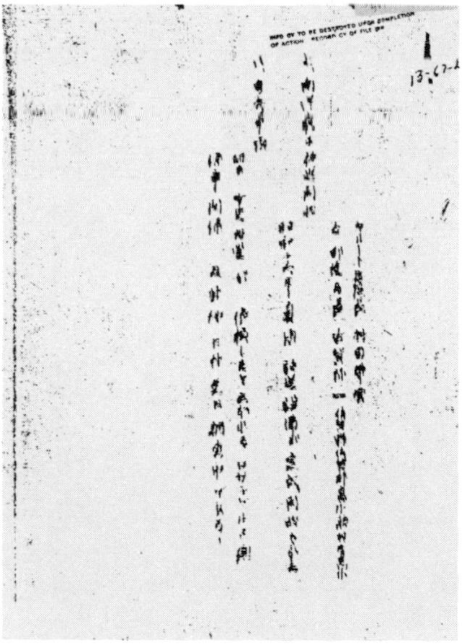

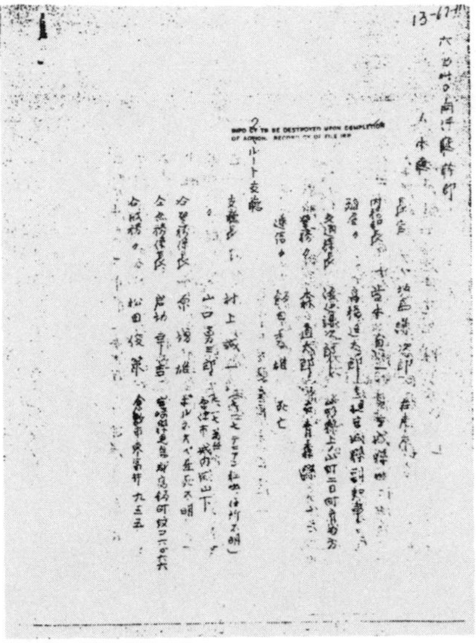

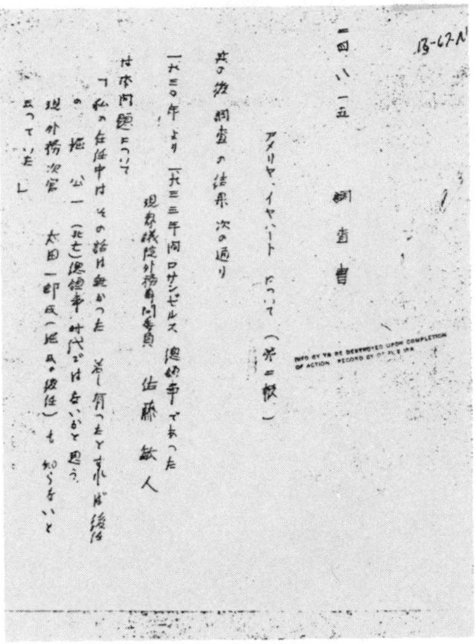

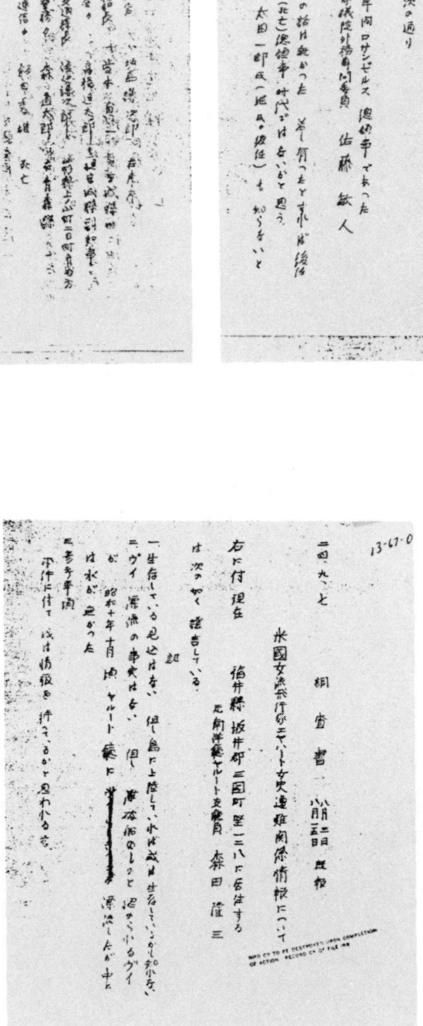

Bibliography

BOOKS

Backus, Jean L. *Letters from Amelia.* Boston: Beacon Press, 1982.

Briand, Paul L., Jr. *Daughter of the Sky.* New York: Duell, Sloan and Pearce, 1960

Brooks-Pazmany, Kathleen. *United States Women in Aviation 1919–1929.* Washington: Smithsonian Institution Press, 1983.

Dwiggins, Don. *Hollywood Pilot.* New York: Doubleday, 1966.

Earhart, Amelia. *Last Flight.* New York: Harcourt, Brace, 1937.

Goerner, Fred. *The Search for Amelia Earhart.* New York: Doubleday, 1966.

Holmes, W. J. *Double-Edged Secrets.* Annapolis, Md.: Naval Institute Press, 1979.

Moolman, Valerie, and editors. *Women Aloft.* Alexandria, Va.: Time Life Books, 1981.

Pellegreno, Ann Holtgren. *World Flight.* Ames, Iowa: Iowa State University Press, 1971. (This book contains a great deal of valuable information on investigations of previous researchers into the Earhart mystery.)

Putnam, George Palmer. *Soaring Wings.* New York: Harcourt, Brace, 1939.

Smith, Elinor. *Aviatrix.* New York: Harcourt Brace Jovanovich, 1981.

Strippel, Dick. *Amelia Earhart: The Myth and the Reality.* Jericho, N.Y.: Exposition Press, 1972.

Thaden, Louise. *High, Wide and Frightened.* New York: Air Facts Press, 1973.

Toland, John. *The Rising Sun.* New York: Random House, 1970.

Zacharias, Ellis M. *Secret Missions.* New York: Putnam, 1946.

MAGAZINE ARTICLES

Aoki, Fukiko. "Was A. Earhart Executed?" *Bungeishunju* magazine, 1983.

Gwynn-Jones, Terry. "Amelia—The Jigsaw is Falling Into Place." *Paradise*, no. 8 (November 1977).

Holbrook, Francis X. "Amelia Earhart's Final Flight." *Proceedings*, Naval Institute Press, 1971.

Riley, Arthur A. "Search for Amelia Earhart Narrows." *Air World*, July 1976.

Vaeth, J. Gordon. "What Happened to Amelia Earhart?" *NOAA*, July 1977.

DOCUMENTS

Balfour, Harry J. Letter to Francis X. Holbrook, November 24, 1969.
———. Letter to Dr. Robert Townley, October 19, 1969.

Central Intelligence, G-2, GHQ. "Report on Amelia Earhart." August 8, 1949.

Collopy, James A. Letter to Secretary, Civil Aviation Board, Territory of New Guinea, August 28, 1937, via Francis X. Holbrook.

Cude, T. H. Letters to Francis X. Holbrook, December 15, 1969 and January 14, 1970.

Defense Agency, Japanese Government. Military History Room. Imperial Japanese Navy and diplomatic records.

Detudamo, Buraro. Letter to Paul Rafford, Jr., September 12, 1983.

Dwiggins, Don. Letters and records from personal collection.

Edwards, Phil. National Air and Space Museum. Records and photos.

Flores, Bishop Felix Umberto. Files in Guam containing over two hundred interviews conducted by Father Arnold Bendowske, O.F.M. Cap., of Saipan, with Saipanese who recalled seeing Amelia Earhart or Fred Noonan.

Hirabayashi, Jyuichi. Interview, personal records, photos.

Holbrook, Francis X. Personal records and letters.

Holmes, W. J. Letter, April 14, 1982.

Hooven, Frederick J. "Amelia Earhart's Last Flight." Unpublished manuscript, National Air and Space Museum files, 1982.

Kamoi, Special Service Vessel, Japanese Imperial Navy. Log books, 1935–1938.

Koshu, Special Service Vessel, Japanese Imperial Navy. Log books, 1937.

Lexington Group. "Report of Earhart Search." USS *Lexington*, July 1937.

Lodeesen, Captain Marius. "The Hero Game" (unpublished manuscript).
———. Letters to Paul Rafford, Jr.

LST 836. U.S. Navy ship. Log books, September 1952.

Mitchell, John H. "The Morning Amelia Earhart Ran Out of Luck." Unpublished manuscript, 1983.

National Air and Space Museum, Smithsonian Institution. Amelia Earhart files.

———. C. B. Allen Collection, care of Paul Garber.

———. "Amelia Earhart—Flight Into Yesterday." Symposium featuring Muriel Earhart Morrissey, Fay Gillis Wells, Rear Admiral Richard B. Black, USNR (Ret.), Elgen Long, Frederick Goerner, Gordon Vaeth. 1982.

National Archives and Records Service. CAA records, diplomatic records, U.S. Coast Guard files, old Army and USN records.

Nuclear Test Personnel Review. USN, USAF records and logs, Operation Ivy, 1952.

Papua (New Guinea), National Library. Records and papers on Amelia Earhart.

Purdue University. Amelia Earhart Collection, Box 1.(5)[3].

Putnam, George Palmer. Letter to Paul Mantz, June 3, 1937, via Don Dwiggins.

Rafford, Paul, Jr. "Amelia Earhart—Her Own Navigator?" Unpublished manuscript, 1983.

Sexton, Irene. Letter to Francis X. Holbrook, December 31, 1969.

Shear, Dellwyn. The British Phosphate Commission, Nauru. Letter to Francis X. Holbrook, August 29, 1969.

Shimkus, Robert. Taped recollections, expedition to Marshall Islands.

U.S. Coast Guard. Office of the Historian. *Itasca* records, Amelia Earhart file.

Washburn, Bradford. "Amelia Earhart's Last Flight." Unpublished manuscript, interview, 1983.

Webb, Patricia Thaden. Interview, records, documents (1983).

Western Electric Company. Letters and telegrams (1937), via Don Dwiggins.

Wolfe, Frank H., Jr. "Analysis of the Last Amelia Earhart Flight." Unpublished manuscript, National Air and Space Museum Earhart files.

Index

About the Authors

VINCENT V. LOOMIS is a former USAF Officer with two tours of duty in the North and South Pacific to his credit. He has been awarded the Distinguished Flying Cross and the Air Medal and has served as Official Pilot for the White House Staff. Mr. Loomis established, and was Commanding Officer of, the first down range station, Grand Bahama Island of the Eastern Missile Test Range, and was the "Operations Officer" on Eniwetok, Marshall Islands, during "Operation Ivy," the first H-bomb test.

During Mr. Loomis' tour in the Marshall Islands, he discovered an airplane he believes was the one flown by Amelia Earhart. He led six expeditions to the North and South Pacific and Japan in order to determine what happened to Amelia Earhart and Fred Noonan after their flight around the world in 1937. Mr. Loomis is also executive producer of a film documentary based on his Earhart expeditions.

JEFFREY ETHELL has been writing about aviation subjects since 1967, authoring hundreds of magazine articles and over 20 books. Learning to fly before learning to drive a car, he holds numerous pilots ratings and regularly flies current high performance aircraft with the USAF, USN, USMC and several foreign air forces. He is qualified to fly a variety of aircraft, including such World War II types as the P-51 Mustang and B-25 Mitchell. His recent books include *Air War South Atlantic, Fox Two, Pilot Maker* and *P-38 Lightning.*